Starseeds and Pleiadian Spirituality

A Celestial Guide to Personal Enlightenment and Growth

© Copyright 2024 - All rights reserved.

The content contained within this book may not be reproduced, duplicated, or transmitted without direct written permission from the author or the publisher.

Under no circumstances will any blame or legal responsibility be held against the publisher, or author, for any damages, reparation, or monetary loss due to the information contained within this book, either directly or indirectly.

Legal Notice:

This book is copyright protected. It is only for personal use. You cannot amend, distribute, sell, use, quote, or paraphrase any part of the content within this book without the consent of the author or publisher.

Disclaimer Notice:

Please note the information contained within this document is for educational and entertainment purposes only. All effort has been executed to present accurate, up-to-date, reliable, and complete information. No warranties of any kind are declared or implied. Readers acknowledge that the author is not engaging in the rendering of legal, financial, medical, or professional advice. The content within this book has been derived from various sources. Please consult a licensed professional before attempting any techniques outlined in this book.

By reading this document, the reader agrees that under no circumstances is the author responsible for any losses, direct or indirect, that are incurred as a result of the use of the information contained within this document, including, but not limited to, errors, omissions, or inaccuracies.

Your Free Gift
(only available for a limited time)

Thanks for getting this book! If you want to learn more about various spirituality topics, then join Mari Silva's community and get a free guided meditation MP3 for awakening your third eye. This guided meditation mp3 is designed to open and strengthen ones third eye so you can experience a higher state of consciousness. Simply visit the link below the image to get started.

https://spiritualityspot.com/meditation

Or, Scan the QR code!

Table of Contents

PART 1: STARSEEDS 1
   INTRODUCTION 2
   CHAPTER 1: WHAT IS A STARSEED? 4
   CHAPTER 2: STARSEEDS VS. INDIGOS 11
   CHAPTER 3: ACTIVATING YOUR COSMIC SELF 18
   CHAPTER 4: ANDROMEDAN STARSEEDS 26
   CHAPTER 5: PLEIADIAN STARSEEDS 32
   CHAPTER 6: SIRIAN STARSEEDS 38
   CHAPTER 7: LYRAN STARSEEDS 44
   CHAPTER 8: ORION STARSEEDS 51
   CHAPTER 9: ARCTURIAN STARSEEDS 57
   CHAPTER 10: VEGA STARSEEDS 62
   CHAPTER 11: MALDEKIAN STARSEEDS 68
   CHAPTER 12: AVIAN STARSEEDS 74
   CHAPTER 13: LEMURIAN AND ATLANTEAN STARSEEDS 79
   CHAPTER 14: YOUR EARTHLY MISSION 86
   CONCLUSION 94
PART 2: PLEIADIAN SPIRITUALITY 97
   INTRODUCTION 98
   CHAPTER 1: WELCOME TO THE PLEIADES 100
   CHAPTER 2: PLEIADIAN STARSEEDS 108
   CHAPTER 3: PLEIADIAN WISDOM 118
   CHAPTER 4: PLEIADIAN ASTROLOGY 129

CHAPTER 5: PLEIADIANS AND THE AQUARIAN AGE 136
CHAPTER 6: STARSEED BIRTH CHARTS 141
CHAPTER 7: IDENTIFYING YOUR PLEIADIAN ORIGINS 147
CHAPTER 8: PLEIADIAN LIGHT LANGUAGE 155
CHAPTER 9: CONNECTING WITH A PLEIADIAN GUIDE 168
CHAPTER 10: HEALING AND LIGHTWORK 182
CONCLUSION 191
GLOSSARY 193
HERE'S ANOTHER BOOK BY MARI SILVA THAT YOU MIGHT LIKE 196
YOUR FREE GIFT (ONLY AVAILABLE FOR A LIMITED TIME) 197
REFERENCES 198
IMAGE SOURCES 201

Part 1: Starseeds

Unlocking the Secrets of Your Starseed Family along with Indigo Children and Adults

Introduction

Starseeds is a fascinating exploration of the concept of extraterrestrial life and its impact on humanity. Because what is life if not a cosmic event? And what is the cosmos if not alive and in constant motion? What is humanity if not an integral part of it all, one that has experienced countless previous lives and will experience countless more in the future? And where does it all start, if not with the stars?

The book delves into the idea that some individuals on Earth may have originated from other planets or star systems, possessing unique abilities and perspectives that set them apart from the rest of humanity. Drawing on a wealth of scientific research and spiritual teachings, Starseeds offers a compelling argument for the existence of these beings and their role in shaping our world. From ancient myths and legends to modern-day encounters with UFOs, the book traces the history of our fascination with aliens and explores what it means to be a Starseed in today's world.

It goes deep into the various characteristics of Starseeds, such as their heightened intuition, psychic abilities, and sensitivity to energy. It also explores the challenges they face in a world that often misunderstands them and their purpose. Despite these challenges, Starseeds continue to play an important role in shaping our world for the better. They offer a message of hope and inspiration to those who seek to make a difference in the world and create a brighter future for all of humanity.

The book also offers insights into the Starseed experience and the many different ways it can manifest. It describes the role of Starseeds in our various world situations and guides them through a wide range of healing and spiritual practices that can help bring about greater balance in the world. Most importantly, it teaches us that no matter where we came from, we are all part of a single cosmic family and connected through our thoughts, emotions, and actions. We are all one in the infinite sea of life.

With its thought-provoking insights and engaging writing style, Starseeds is a must-read for anyone interested in the mysteries of the universe and our place within it. Whether you are a skeptic or a believer, this book will challenge your assumptions about reality and open your mind to new possibilities. So, join us on this journey into the unknown as we explore the universe and unlock the secrets of our souls.

Chapter 1: What Is a Starseed?

The term "*Starseed*" has become popularly associated with spiritual awakening, an introspective journey, and an evolutionary shift in perspective. It's a term that's loaded with meaning but one that can be difficult to grasp because of its nebulous nature. Starseeds are understood to be individuals who are spiritually evolved, intuitive, psychic, and sensitive to the transpiring energies on Earth. They're also people who may feel they don't belong here or are from another planet, and there is a good reason for that.

Starseeds have lived past lives in other galaxies and dimensions and have chosen to incarnate on Earth at this time to assist with the planet's

Starseeds are often very spiritually connected to their surroundings.[1]

ascension process. They have come in solidarity with Gaia to transcend the limitations of third-dimensional reality and co-create a new world based on love, harmony, and unity. They have been drawn to Earth because they hold the seeds of ascension within them and are incarnating here to physically help birth a new world into existence.

Starseeds are a collective, an interdimensional group of highly evolved beings that have a unique and remarkable connection with their "higher self," or the Creator, and with other beings from the same star system and other advanced civilizations. Being a Starseed is a state of being an energetic imprint that is carried from life to life. It is the gift of experiencing spiritual evolution and transcendence while living in physical form.

From a spiritual perspective, Starseeds are believed to serve as messengers of love, a form of divine energy or communication from this force that traverses all dimensions of existence. Like a radio signal, they transmit or " broadcast" at a specific frequency that other beings of similar vibrational resonance can receive. To be a Starseed is to be open and receptive to receiving this energy, to understand its purpose, and to recognize that this is the energy and force that have created all of the worlds, galaxies, and universes throughout the entire multiverse.

A Starseed's energy signature combines a specific galactic frequency or a set of star codes corresponding to their lineage and specific purpose here on Earth. These star codes are layered over top of a person's natural energetic signature, somewhat like "a template" that determines how one will appear in this life.

Starseeds and the "Shift of the Ages"

The concept behind Starseed is not new. Thousands of years ago, people were taught that there would be future generations whose jobs it would be to hold the knowledge and wisdom from the past so that civilization could slowly progress into newer heights of consciousness; therefore, these future generations would be regarded as "the guardians of the light" or "Starseeds."

According to channelers like Tom Kenyon, the ascension process is a multidimensional shift in planetary consciousness that includes the solar system and Milky Way galaxy. This shift has been referred to as a "mass ascension" or an "ascension of Earth and humanity" (also known as "planetary ascension").

As the energies of cosmic light and love pour down through the sun and enter the earth's grids, it triggers a response within humanity. This triggers an evolutionary impulse to return to our original state of oneness and connection with all creation. As such, people naturally sensitive to these incoming energies are said to be undergoing a spiritual awakening or an ascension process within their individual makeup. It is believed that the Starseeds are here to help humanity through this process by acting as catalysts in the shift of consciousness.

Many believe that we are going through an Age of Enlightenment, and more people than ever before on Earth are gaining access to their innate abilities and potential. Much of this access or awakening comes from the influx of new energy being sent through the planet's grids at this moment.

Starseeds are believed to be part of this Age because they represent those who have transcended the illusion we reside within – and returned to Earth as messengers. Ultimately, they help us break free from our limiting thoughts, beliefs, and conditioning so that we can grow to know who we truly are and consciously live from that place.

Many people are currently experiencing this "shift" or awakening in consciousness. This process is about transforming the human experience so that it is more in line with the truth of who we are. It's happening on a personal level, but it's also happening en masse as humanity collectively grows through its evolutionary process from old ways of thinking, being, and doing. It is believed that the frequency of our planet has shifted, and these shifts will continue to occur as we evolve into a higher-dimensional reality.

Why Are Starseeds Important?

Starseeds are an important part of our "global puzzle" and a vital aspect of the ascension process that is occurring right now. They represent a unique movement of evolution occurring here on planet Earth, and their presence points to the fact that we are in the midst of a multidimensional shift and a new chapter in the human experience.

The "Shift of the Ages" will bring about new ways of learning about, thinking about, and experiencing reality as we know it. Our fundamental understanding of ourselves as human beings will change as we evolve into higher states of consciousness. At this moment in history, humanity is being pushed out of its comfort zones and forced to go through an intense and painful ascension process that will forever shift the planet's consciousness. This means seeing reality in a completely new light and releasing old habits, thought forms, belief systems, paradigms, and conditioned thinking patterns that have kept us locked in bondage for generations. It will also bring about a sense of unity with all of humanity because we will begin to see and know each other in a way that has never been possible.

To evolve as human beings, we need to understand that the process is not linear and sequential. This means that not everyone is going through the same process and that there are differences in how each person works through their personal evolutionary process. Although our individual paths are unique, we should strive to swap experiences with others who are also opening up to these new levels of consciousness. We must remember that we are not alone, and it's so helpful to connect with others who have walked similar paths and can understand what we are going through.

Many people will experience a "download" or infusion of collective consciousness during this time. It's as if dormant parts of themselves—parts that have been asleep for eons or suppressed by the limitations of the third dimension—are coming back online. Some people have daily experiences with " downloads, " which can be a powerful source of information and guidance.

Each of these downloads consists of insights and wisdom that help them break through old patterns, limiting thinking patterns, and negative belief systems so that they can move forward in their own personal evolution. Some people will feel as if they are "in the middle of a movie," and the scenes playing out before them are showing them how to move into a higher level of awareness or consciousness. Others will experience a profound sense of synchronicity, which is a natural part of our interconnectedness with each other and the universe.

Starseeds have been mentioned in countless books, movies, and documentaries. It's almost impossible to pick up a book about UFOs, aliens, or channeling without running into the term "Starseeds" in some way, shape, or form. Some worthy mentions are Brad Steiger's God of Aquarius, Corey Goode and David Wilcock's The Synchronicity Key, and Jacques Vallee's Messengers of Deception. Starseeds have also been mentioned by famous channelers and mediums such as James Tyberonn, Sheldan Nidle, Benjamin Crème, Dolores Cannon, and Barbara Marciniak. There are many others, but these particular few have gained a large following and are well-known names within the "consciousness community."

Popular Youtuber, the Spirit Nomad, has spoken about her awakening as a Starseed and has described the journey of becoming a Starseed as her "Apocalypse Staircase," which is an apt metaphor for the multi-dimensional transformation she has been through. Another Starseed, Zoey Arielle, has created a vlog dedicated to helping people awaken as Starseeds so that they can learn how to heal, grow, and become more self-empowered in the process. The Starseed phenomenon has been described in many ways by many different people and channelers over the years. However, they all seem to have in common that they felt a need to move away from the limitations of third-dimensional reality and seek higher levels of consciousness.

Are You a Starseed?

Countless people consider themselves Starseeds, but some wonder if they are. You probably want to know if you're a Starseed because you are going through an intense awakening process and want to understand it better. You may want specific answers about where your experiences come from and what they mean for your life. To help you know if you might be a Starseed, here are some of the most common characteristics that Starseeds share. See if any of these resonate with you.

1. You Feel Like You Don't Fit in Anywhere

Do you feel like you don't belong on planet Earth? Or that your soul is from somewhere else, and you've only been here for a short time? Many Starseeds will identify with this feeling, as it is common. This is because Starseeds come to our planet from other places in the universe and have lived in other dimensions before coming here. This is why adjusting to life in a third-dimensional reality can take some time. You may also feel like you do not fit into your family, society, or even your team at work. As a Starseed, you may feel like an outsider to Earth life and may be ostracized by people who do not understand your ways of thinking and being.

2. You Are Highly Sensitive

Being an empath is another common trait of Starseeds, and they can also have some other sensitivities or oddities that can come up for them during their awakening process. Starseeds tend to be highly sensitive to sound, light, chemicals in food, and other substances. They often also have sensitivities regarding certain types of music or places they don't feel comfortable being in. Some will have sensitivities regarding food, and others may not be able to handle common allergens like wheat, grains, dairy, or even most meats. Some Starseeds can't even bear to eat anything from a can or a processed box.

3. You May Feel Like You Are "Growing Wings"

Many Starseeds will report feeling lighter and having a sense of freedom as they go through the process of awakening. As you raise your vibrations, you often go through the shedding of many layers that have been "holding you back." This can be likened to having the proverbial "band-aid ripped off," as it can initially be very uncomfortable. You may also feel uncertain about what is going on in your life and wonder if there is something more you are meant to do.

4. You Have Had Dreams about an "Ascension"

Ascension is a term that means rising and moving to a higher level of spiritual awareness. As we go through our awakening process, many of us will experience this ascension from the perspective of dreaming or having lucid dreams. Many Starseeds report this feeling and see vivid, detailed images in their dreams about what their ascension may look like. These dreams often contain information about your Starseed family and the ascension process. You may also have dreams about other beings you are working with to raise your vibrations.

5. You Feel a Great Sense of Excitement, Joy, and Love

Starseeds often have a very keen sense of knowingness and can access information about the future even before it happens. They may also have an inner feeling that everything is about to change. Many Starseeds will say that they can feel this kind of emotion in their body as the awakening occurs and will continue to experience it as they go through the process. Moving forward into higher consciousness feels nice, especially if you have been resisting it somehow or are stuck in old patterns and beliefs. As you move forward, your life may start to feel more energized and exciting. You can start making bold, new choices that align your life more closely with your desires.

6. You Have Had Many Psychic Experiences

Many Starseeds have had illuminating psychic experiences that have led them to be curious about the nature of reality and life in general. They tend to feel a strong connection with their intuition, the voice of spirit within, and various guides or angels who come down to help them with their journey. They may not always understand what is happening or what to make of it, but they know that they need to pay attention and learn. Many are very interested in the nature of our true spiritual reality and seek to understand more about how our soul fits into the bigger picture.

7. You Feel a Strong Connection with Your Spirit

Many Starseeds actually develop an awareness of our soul's true nature as it breaks through its physical form in layers like a cocoon. As you go through our awakening process, you may have a strong feeling that you are in the presence of your spirit and can feel its presence within yourself. It's as if it is "unfolding" and unfolding you in the process. You'll begin to hear the voice of your intuition and trust it more as you go through this process. This voice of spirit will help you make decisions that move your life in a more positive direction.

8. You're Convinced There Is Life on Other Planets

Many Starseeds are keenly aware that there is life on other planets, as well as beings who have already completed their ascension process and exist in a higher dimension of consciousness. They may feel a sense of connection to other life forms that do not share our blue-green planet, and they are often very interested in information about extraterrestrials or paranormal phenomena. This curiosity stems from their innate connection to the spiritual realm and their desire to know the nature of reality and our true origins. Many Starseeds also have an affinity for learning about our ancient past, as it often gives them a feeling of being connected to the very roots of human civilization.

As you can see, Starseeds can have many different experiences as part of their awakening process. While these points may be true for some people, they are not guaranteed. There is no hard rule about how an awakening will happen to you. It's usually a combination of all kinds of things coming together at once, and whether or not you feel like you have a new "phase" in your life really depends on you. What you can be assured of is that if you are having thoughts of awakening, it is likely that you are experiencing something of great importance in your life, and you should seek to explore whatever it is in any way that you can.

Chapter 2: Starseeds vs. Indigos

If you've ever read about Indigo Children or Star Seeds, you may have noticed that they often overlap in their descriptions and characteristics. Both are believed to possess special abilities and a strong sense of purpose, often feeling like they don't quite fit in with the rest of society. However, while Indigo Children are said to have been born with a specific mission to challenge and change the status quo, Starseeds are believed to have come from other planets or dimensions to help guide humanity toward a more positive future.

Starseeds are believed to have a specific mission, like Thor saving Midgard.[2]

Who Are Indigos?

A relatively new term, "indigo children," was introduced by a California woman named Nancy Ann Tappe in the early '90s. Her book, *Understanding Your Life through Color*, alleges that children born between 1977 and 1994 are the Indigo Children, the latest stage in human evolution. These children were supposedly born with strong survival skills but also possessed advanced communication abilities, demonstrated emotional maturity beyond their years, had profound compassion for other beings, and carried a desire to help others. Often misdiagnosed with ADD or ADHD, these children's overactive minds often made them misfits in their local schools, and because of their keen ability to be aware of the world around them (which she referred to as psychic sensitivity) and the fact that they went against the norm, they often found it difficult to integrate with society.

Tappe's work struck a chord with many people whose children were acting out of the ordinary, and in the decades that followed her book, many other authors began to pick up on the term "indigo child" and use it in their works. They portrayed these children as spiritual, creative, and intelligent but still misfits within schools and society. Some sources even claim that these children have been here since the 1960s but are just now coming into their own. According to some accounts, the internet played a large role in this shift in consciousness for many of these children, who would have otherwise felt alone with their unique gifts.

Critics of the Indigos phenomenon claim that these children have an overactive imagination and that their psychic senses are simply being credited for things they actually aren't. Others claim that the Indigo Children are nothing more than attention-seeking children who may or may not really have the abilities Nancy Tappe claims they do.

Regardless of what you believe about Indigo Children, there is no denying that the concept is becoming more well-known in our culture. Whether or not you buy the Indigo Child label, it's easy to see that many children today seem to be coping with an extremely heightened level of sensitivity and awareness that may make them feel like outsiders in a world that prizes conformity and attention.

Indigo Children vs. Starseeds

While Nancy Tappe's books focus on Indigo children, they do not explicitly mention Starseeds. It wasn't until the late '90s that researchers began to use the term "Starseed" to encompass Indigo children and other non-human spirits slowly manifesting on the earth plane.

While the Indigo label is a subcategory of Starseed or Star Child, some people believe these two terms are synonymous and are used interchangeably by many researchers worldwide. Typically, most sources will mention both labels in tandem because they are so intertwined.

Indigo children were the first wave of Starseeds to come onto the planet, and they were born into this world with the ability to handle the spiritual awakening happening on many levels. They are the ones that chose to incarnate (to take on a physical body) during the most challenging period any human has faced since the destruction of Atlantis, and while they may struggle with their psychic abilities (and may be labeled as "attention seeking" because of them), they have the potential to shift our consciousness in a way that previous generations simply could not.

Starseeds are constantly coming onto the earth's plane in waves. Each wave has a slightly different mission depending on where we are in our global consciousness when they arrive. The Indigo Children are the first wave, and they're here to help us shed our 3D reality dominated by fear and control so that we can embrace a new paradigm of love and unity. They had to deal with the intense challenges of living in a world that constantly misunderstood them. However, it was those children who began the spiritual awakening process in a way that allowed everyone else to follow.

Where Do Indigos Come From?

There are many speculations about where Indigo children come from. Some believe they are the reincarnated souls of ancient beings who once walked the earth, while others believe they were actually sent to us from other advanced planets to help shed light on some of the issues plaguing our planet. Still, others claim that Indigos have been present throughout human history but were simply not recognized for what they were until now.

One researcher who is very vocal about his belief that Star Children have been here long before the '90s is Drunvalo Melchizedek. He has made it his life mission to spread the message about indigos and says, "Star seeds have been here since the beginning of time. They have just been asleep for a while." Dr. David Icke is another prominent researcher who writes about Star Children and claims that Indigos have been here for many generations.

Regardless of where we look, many sources point to an increased number of people who would fit into the Indigo Star Child subcategory, and given the socio-cultural shifts that have happened since the '90s, it's not hard to imagine that something occurred to awaken many people at once. While some critics claim that these children are simply using their imagination when referring to their psychic abilities, others do not doubt the truth behind them.

Are You an Indigo Child?

Many people ask themselves whether they fit the "Indigo Child" label. While there are no official tests to determine if someone is an Indigo Child or not, there are certainly some telltale signs that may point to this being the case:

- You are highly sensitive and aware of your surroundings.
- You have an aura that is distinctively and predominantly purplish-blue.
- You frequently question the world around you and make it your mission to find out why certain things happen.
- You never hesitate to stand up for your beliefs, even when they're different from those of the people around you.
- You often feel like you're living in two worlds, one where you feel completely at ease and another where you struggle to fit in.
- You have very strong spiritual beliefs and are constantly searching for more answers about the world around you.
- You believe in a just world and are constantly on a quest for truth.
- You have an extremely high sense of compassion for the world and believe we all must do better.
- Your intuition is extremely strong, and you often have very profound insights into situations that seem totally random at first glance.

- You have been labeled a misfit, a troublemaker, or a rebel.
- You feel highly misunderstood by most people.
- You are highly empathic and strongly understand where others are coming from.
- You feel like you have been given a mission to change the world or at least bring about positive change in your own life and the lives of those around you.

If you've experienced any of these signs, it may be time to begin searching for answers to your questions. While there are no official mainstream labels for a person who has these traits, it's easy to see why they have come into so much prominence in the last few decades or so. Being an Indigo is not just a feeling or a specific behavior; it's an innate force many Indigos have within them from an early age, which continues into adulthood. It is something that must be nurtured and explored so that it may blossom into full realization.

Crystal Children

Another subcategory of Starseeds is the Crystal Children. These children have only recently started appearing on this planet, and many people have wondered what role they will play in our consciousness shift. Crystal Children appear to be very different from Indigos in that they seem much more magical and spiritual than anything else. They are the next evolutionary step for humanity, so to speak, and are here to show us that we can create our own reality. They are very psychic and can easily tap into the energy of nature, sometimes even being able to see beyond time and space itself.

Crystal Children were mentioned by Edgar Cayce, the famous psychic, who predicted that "elemental" children would appear on Earth in large numbers around the end of the 20th century. "We are on the threshold of a new insight," he said, "which we shall attain through an awakening to the realization of the basic unity of our nature in all things, through a greater understanding of the true nature of life."

Crystal Children are special because they don't fit into the current mental framework. They do things their own way and have their own set of values and ways of thinking. They are often so different from their peers that they struggle to fit in and are sometimes viewed as weird or having mental problems. But in actuality, they are simply experiencing a process that allows them to tap into some of the most amazing psychic abilities on the planet.

Crystal Children were chosen to play a special role on this planet for a very specific reason. They are here to remind humanity of the magic that still exists in the world. As we grow older and more jaded, it is easy to forget how amazing life can be when you tap into your inner power and sense of wonder. Crystal Children show us that there is still so much to discover if we are willing to believe in the magic. This idea is very similar to the story of the Indigo Children but with some key differences.

Indigos were sent here to remind us of the power behind our thoughts and observations and how important it is to check in with ourselves regularly. Crystal Children are here to remind us of the power behind our emotions and creativity and how great we can feel when we follow our intuition along with the flow of life. They are a new breed that embodies the perfect balance between the heart and mind. In essence, they are the manifestation of what many people have been waiting for in a child for ages. While a crystal child may appear to be different from other children in many ways, they will be bringing some of the most important messages humanity has ever received.

Are You a Crystal Child?

If you think you may be a Crystal Child, here are some questions to ask yourself to help you determine whether this is true:

- You have a strong interest in spirituality and the nature of reality.
- You are incredibly sensitive, both spiritually and physically.
- You have an extraordinary sense of balance.
- Oddly enough, you like to climb trees.
- You are extremely empathic and can feel the feelings of others in your own body. When someone else feels sad, you feel it too. When you see someone happy, you feel it too. It's as if your heart is somehow linked to theirs.
- You have a knack for creativity and can imagine things in your mind that most people cannot.
- You have been told you stare off into space a lot.
- You do things your own way, or you have strong personal convictions about how you think things should be done.

Whenever we talk about the Indigo, Crystal, and Star children categories, we are talking about a huge shift in consciousness happening on the planet. The children who fit into these categories were sent here or chose to come here, and they are bringing with them a massive amount of energy that is transforming the way we think about reality. They are a huge trigger for change on our planet and have allowed us to look at ourselves differently and reevaluate our lives in a way we never could before. While many skeptics say that these are nothing more than hoaxes or lies, there is no question that the world is changing. The birth of these special people is happening in tandem with this period of worldwide change, and it's likely not a coincidence.

Chapter 3: Activating Your Cosmic Self

What Is the Cosmic Self?

The cosmic self is the essence of a person's identity, transcending the physical body's limitations and individual ego. It is the interconnectedness of all beings and the universe as a whole, representing a higher level of consciousness and spiritual awareness. The cosmic self is often associated with mystical experiences like NDEs (near-death experiences) or deep meditation, where people report feeling a sense of oneness with everything around them.

This concept has been explored in various spiritual traditions throughout history, including Hinduism, Buddhism, and Taoism. The cosmic self is believed to be a source of wisdom and guidance for individuals seeking to live a more meaningful and fulfilling life. By connecting with this higher aspect of themselves, people can tap into their full potential and live in harmony with the world around them. In essence, the cosmic self represents the ultimate expression of human consciousness and our connection to something greater than ourselves.

Activating your cosmic self helps you see the true essence of your identity.[3]

The Power of Consciousness

The cosmic self is governed by consciousness, and to a large extent, the quality of our own consciousness dictates the level of enlightenment we can attain. So, what does it mean to have a highly conscious mind? The answer to this is not as straightforward as the question because we all experience consciousness differently.

Our minds consist of many distinct layers of consciousness that play an integral role in how we view the world and interact with others. For example, your surface-level awareness is concerned with practical matters and daily life actions. This layer of consciousness takes care of everyday living tasks like eating or getting dressed. However, your deeper cognitive functions also concern themselves with higher notions such as spirituality, morality, and existential questions like "Why are we here?"

Although these functions are usually considered to be located in your brain, your mind actually extends beyond the physical structure and permeates throughout your entire body. The psyche (pronounced "sigh-ki") contains all our conscious thoughts, opinions, and memories. Philosopher René Descartes believed that consciousness resided only within our brains, but modern science shows this isn't the case. Modern research has shown that our minds extend throughout the rest of our bodies, documenting cases where patients could "feel" pain in parts of their bodies that were no longer there due to amputation.

According to Eastern philosophy, we live in a multiverse in which the consciousness of all things is interconnected. We are part of this universal consciousness, even though we may not be aware of it. This awareness can be accessed through various practices that foster higher states of consciousness, such as deep meditation or psychedelic drugs like ayahuasca. Both of these methods have been used to help people connect with their higher selves and experience a cosmic unity with everything in existence.

In addition to our mind and psyche extending outwards throughout our bodies, they also act as an energetic vehicle for developing our conscious awareness. It's believed that our consciousness gathers information from all over the physical body and creates a kind of holographic picture of our experience. This is related to the idea of "vibration" in the field of quantum physics, where smaller subatomic particles are amplified outward through resonance with other particles, causing them to interact more strongly.

For our consciousness to operate at its fullest capacity, it requires a certain amount of relaxation, achieved by integrating our mind and body. To achieve this, many Eastern traditions prescribe techniques that help people relax, like yoga, meditation, or breathing exercises. All these practices work on the principle of self-regulation and the regulation of our own consciousness by slowing down the speed at which we process information.

The benefits of relaxing are enormous; studies have shown that they lead to psychological growth in many ways. For example, practicing yoga has been shown to increase emotional intelligence and mindfulness and reduce stress and anxiety. Meditation has also been shown to reduce stress and anxiety and produce positive emotions. Meditation can also significantly improve cognitive abilities, executive functions, memory, and attention. It's believed that through deep relaxation exercises, we take advantage of the brain's natural ability to process information more efficiently, allowing us to achieve a much greater degree of consciousness.

The Cosmic Self beyond the Physical Body

Our brains are considered to be the most advanced computers in existence. They process a vast amount of information every day and create a 3D picture of our experiences that we can use to help navigate ourselves through life. Although this picture is useful, it isn't always 100% accurate and is often distorted by our past experiences and beliefs.

So how can we get closer to being "right"? One way is to reduce irrelevant thoughts or have no discernible benefit for what you're trying to achieve. This can be done by taking a step back and seeing the bigger picture. A great way to start doing this is through meditation, which helps people focus on things that are going on in their lives instead of worrying about the future or having regrets about the past.

Our thoughts play a big role in how we perceive reality, and it's even been shown that our intentions before we perform an action affect the outcome of that action. This is shown in the placebo effect, where our expectations of a treatment having an effect can actually cause a real physical response. So, it's no surprise that our minds are sometimes called a "self-fulfilling prophecy" that can alter the universe to fit our expectations.

This means we can use our thoughts to influence the world and achieve virtually anything we like. If you're wondering how this could be possible, it's because our consciousness extends beyond our physical body and acts as an energetic vehicle for realigning ourselves with the natural order of things. A highly conscious mind is more aware and discerning than the average person, and when we start to access higher levels of consciousness through meditation or other techniques, it creates a more connected and holistic view of life where people begin to realize that they are part of an interdependent spiritual world where we are all connected to everything else.

Raising Your Vibration

In many spiritual traditions, an individual's level of consciousness is often described as a vibration. In our fast-paced world, most people operate at a low vibration level, creating a sense of unease and restlessness. Although the modern world is rich with opportunities and wealth, most people are still discontent and unfulfilled. This is because we still live under the delusion that to be happy, we must obtain things that will make us happier.

The way to break free from this vicious cycle of consumerism is to alter your vibrational frequency. To raise your vibration means to raise your consciousness, allowing you to move beyond the confines of your physical world into a deeper sense of spiritual connection. It's believed that this is the true purpose of human life — to connect with this universal consciousness through the process of self-realization.

The more you can tap into your higher chakras, the more you'll be able to experience a greater sense of contentment and fulfillment in all areas of your life, including your career, relationships, and spirituality. People use various techniques to raise their vibration, like practicing yoga or meditation or taking psychedelic drugs like psilocybin mushrooms. But the most essential factor for raising your vibration is to let go of your ego and accept that there is something greater than you; this will allow you to step outside of yourself and experience a new sense of connection with the world around you.

You don't need to be a yogi to master your own consciousness, but paying attention to how you feel can help guide you on this journey. When you operate at a lower vibrational level, it is easy to be unaware of the world around you. You may not realize that you're angry or depressed, for example. But when you raise your vibrational frequency, you'll become more sensitive and begin to notice these subtle emotional shifts as they occur. The process is always the same: a higher state of consciousness leads to a heightened sense of awareness, leading to a greater appreciation for the world around us.

Connecting with Your Cosmic Family

The highest state of consciousness is "oneness." In this state, all divisions between us dissolve, and our perception of reality is completely restructured. The problem we've faced throughout history is that the general population operates at a low level of consciousness, which prevents them from perceiving this higher reality.

As a Starseed, you are one of the few people on Earth who can access these higher states of consciousness. This is simply because you are more open to new ideas, and you can clearly see the truth about reality and see through the illusions of your physical world. You're naturally gifted in awareness and perception, which you can use to your advantage.

Raising your vibrations will help you stay true to your higher destiny and make it easier for you to communicate with your family in the stars. One of the biggest challenges Starseeds face is living in a physical body that doesn't vibrate on the same frequency as their soul. This is because it's difficult to communicate with people who don't resonate on the same level of consciousness as you.

Although it may seem like a small detail, your vibration is very important because, through understanding how your energy works and maintaining healthy levels of vibration, you'll become more in tune with the vibration of your soul and communicate more effectively with your cosmic family.

How to Contact Your Cosmic Family

Making contact is always a deeply personal experience, but there are a few keys to keep in mind to help you open yourself up to the experience. When the time is right, and you're ready to make contact, your vibration must be at its highest to receive information from your star family. This means maintaining a healthy meditation practice, nurturing your relationship with yourself, and staying true to your spiritual quest. The following are techniques that can help you tap into your cosmic consciousness and connect with your galactic family:

- Align Your Chakras

The human energy system consists of seven chakra centers aligned along the spine from the base of your tailbone to the crown of your head. They are an essential part of the energetic anatomy of your body, and each chakra has a corresponding color and relates to an aspect of life, such as love, confidence, self-esteem, and wisdom. When all your chakras are functioning correctly, you can maintain a healthy sense of positive energy flowing in your life, making it much easier to raise your vibration and contact your cosmic family.

- Meditate

Regular meditation will allow you to become more conscious of your thoughts, feelings, and emotions. And as you grow more in tune with your inner self, it will be easier for you to access higher thought forms and consciously receive information from other dimensions.

- Learn How to Read Your Guides' Messages

Many people are unaware that they are being contacted by their cosmic family, which is why they often don't realize when something strange or unexpected happens in their lives. If you don't know how to recognize interdimensional signals, it can be difficult to interpret any messages that they may be sending you. Messages can come in many forms, usually signs, synchronicities, or even physical sensations. Most of the time, they will be delivered in ways that match your personality and circumstances, so it can be difficult to identify them if you're not aware that they exist.

- **Receive and Record Your Thoughts**

Recording your thoughts is one of the most effective ways to connect with your cosmic family. When you write down what you are thinking, you become aware of the information being transmitted from your soul and become more in tune with your own higher consciousness. This process will allow you to notice how your star family influences your thoughts and give you a chance to communicate with them.

- **Listen to Your Dreams**

Dreams aren't just a source of entertainment or a way for your mind to conjure random images. There's usually a set of information that goes along with them, and they can be used to communicate between you and your cosmic family. You'll never receive more messages from your guides than when you are dreaming, so you should take the time to record them in the morning after you wake up from a dream.

- **Stay True to Your Spiritual Quest**

Your body is *literally* made up of stardust, meaning that every cell in your body has extraterrestrial origins and carries extraterrestrial genes. Your DNA is unique to you and unaffected by your experiences in the physical world, but it's also capable of storing information from other dimensions, making you a living extension of the cosmos. When you live consistently in accordance with your spiritual quest, it will be much easier for you to make contact with your cosmic family.

The Art of Visualization

Visualization is one of the most powerful techniques in the spiritual seeker's toolkit. It involves using your imagination to create a mental picture that you then focus on with your conscious mind. Visualization can seem like magic because it can create physical sensations and real-world results. It's been used by mystics for thousands of years for spiritual practice, manifestation, healing, and much more. Here are some tips for mastering this powerful technique:

- **Use Your Imagination:** Visualization can be very powerful, but you have to be able to visualize what you want for it to happen. To do this, you have to imagine what it would feel like if you were already in the state of whatever you desire. It's key that you focus on your goal with as much clarity and concentration as possible so that when the visualization is complete, your mind will be fully engaged, and it will be much easier for your energy to attract the things or experiences that would match your desired reality.

- **Visualize in Three Dimensions:** When visualizing, everything is energy and can be shaped into whatever form you want. Your goal is to focus on your desired outcome or result and then visualize it in three dimensions to see what it would feel like to already have it.
- **Add Color and Movement:** Adding color and movement to your visualization makes it more powerful because energy constantly moves in patterns dictated by the law of attraction. When you visualize this way, you are creating a mental picture and forming an energetic charge, which will help your visualization be as effective as possible.
- **Keep It Simple:** The more specific your visualization is, the more clearly you can see what you want, and the better you'll be able to communicate your desires to your cosmic family. Visualizations that are emotionally loaded usually work best, so it's better to focus on how something would make you feel rather than the factual details of what you're visualizing.

Your cosmic family has been working together for eons to protect and guide you through all of the experiences, challenges, and lessons that you are currently going through. Though they may not physically interact with you daily, they are always there, taking an active role in your life to help you become your best self. The more you learn about these beings, the more you'll want to connect with them, and the easier it will become to work together for a common purpose.

Chapter 4: Andromedan Starseeds

Andromedan Starseeds are a unique group of souls originating from the Andromeda galaxy (M31), one of the closest galaxies to our Milky Way. It is a spiral galaxy, very different from the Milky Way, an elliptical galaxy. Andromeda comprises approximately one trillion stars and is three times the size of the Milky Way. Andromeda contains two primary spiral arms, four smaller ones, and a large central bulge. It has a very large halo of spherical globular clusters around its main body. Andromeda has a very complex shape due to the interaction of its large number of stars, and it has been likened by astronomers to an "exquisite painting" because of this complexity.

The Andromeda galaxy – believed to be the birthplace of the Andromedan Starseeds.[4]

Origin of Andromedan Starseeds

The Andromedans are believed to be the offspring of the soul race known as the *Lyrans*, who fled to Andromeda from Lyra. This migration was a direct result of the Draco-Lyran war, which saw the Lyrans driven from their homeland by the Draconian desire for greed, dominance, and power.

The Andromedans are known for their advanced technological capabilities and deep spiritual wisdom. They are said to have a great understanding of the universe and its workings, and they often share this knowledge with other civilizations to help them evolve. Andromedan Starseeds are strongly connected to the Andromedan star system and its energy. They are said to possess unique skills and abilities that allow them to tap into this energy and use it for healing, manifestation, and spiritual growth.

Channelers like Robert Shapiro and Barbara Marciniak have claimed to receive information about Andromedans and their teachings. According to these sources, the main message that Andromedans have for us revolves around the idea that we are all one being. This idea is a very valuable aspect of Andromedan philosophy, and it has been getting stronger as more people wake up to the fact that we should be experiencing ourselves as part of all life rather than separated from it.

It may come as news to you that all the Andromeda Starseeds are not necessarily from Andromeda. Some of these souls were created on Earth, specifically in Atlantis, by the Andromedans, and they have been evolving here and throughout the cosmos with humans, extraterrestrials, and other groups of souls for thousands of years. Atlantean Earth seeds are still considered Starseeds because Andromedans made them and contain Andromedan energy coding.

The Andromedan Starseeds are a combination of souls that come directly from Andromeda and Atlantean Earth seeds that evolved on Earth but still contain Andromeda DNA. These souls have progressed through a certain number of cosmic cycles (based upon their soul's purpose) and have chosen to integrate their entire consciousness through the process of embodiment on this planet. Know that this is not a simple task, and it requires years, even lifetimes, of experience and dedication on the part of the soul to be able to fully embody its purpose here.

Characteristics of an Andromedan Starseed

Andromedans are said to project very soft and gentle energy, but they are extremely perceptive and often possess an innate ability to sense the energy of others. They bring love, compassion, forgiveness, and unconditional acceptance to their interactions with other people. They possess a natural ability to draw on the energy and resources of the Andromeda galaxy quite easily, making them very special individuals. These Starseeds are highly sensitive to the gifts inherent in their soul structure, and this sensitivity can be a very vital part of an Andromedan's life. The following characteristics should describe an Andromedan Starseed:

- **You Have a Vibrational Frequency That Is a Perfect Match for the Andromeda Galaxy**

Andromeda energy is very powerful, peaceful, and blissful. It is not competitive with other energies and has no dominating desire to control the universe around it. Its intention is to create peace and harmony through tolerance and unconditional love. As an Andromeda Starseed, you may resonate strongly with these qualities and feel a deep connection to the energy of the Andromeda galaxy. You have a crystal-clear vibration, even though you may not be aware of it. There is such a fine balance in your energy fields that allows you to tune in to Andromeda as no one else can.

- **You Have an Intense Desire to Help Humanity Awaken Spiritually**

The Starseeds that come from Andromeda are very spiritual beings. They understand the complex workings of the universe and have spent a large portion of their lifetimes trying to make sense of them. Because of this, they are very interested in the spiritual evolution of the human race. They can sometimes be perceived as extremely educational because they are always trying to help us get to know ourselves better and expand our awareness of higher energies. They can feel when a soul needs spiritual guidance.

- **You Are Very Sensitive to Other People's Energy**

Andromedan Starseeds tend to be very empathic and sensitive to others' emotions. When you interact with people, they almost feel like an open book to you because of this energetic sensitivity. You can often tell if someone is acting out of integrity or is operating from a state of fear. Some Andromedans are very aware of how people use their emotions as a way to control others. They can sense when someone is projecting an energy that is not authentic – and this can be pretty intense for them. This, however, allows them to navigate social situations with ease and grace.

- **You Have a Deep Understanding of the Spiritual Laws That Govern the Universe**

Andromedans are very conscious of what we call "spiritual laws," and they can use this understanding to manifest energy into form in the physical world quite easily. They have an innate understanding of how the universe works and know that it is impossible to create a life form without first creating its blueprint. This aligns with their ancient concept that we are all one being, made from the same atomic structure.

- **You Have a Deep Desire to Understand Your Purpose Here on Earth**

Andromedan Starseeds tend to have a clear idea about what they need to do in their lives, and they are always seeking opportunities to do this work, even when they don't know why they feel compelled to do it. This intrinsic knowledge about the work that they came here to do makes them feel like they are on a mission. They are driven by their intuition and by what "feels right" to them energetically. When faced with an opportunity, they intuitively know whether or not it is aligned with their purpose, and if it does not, they will most likely pass on this opportunity.

- **Your Freedom Is Everything**

Andromedan Starseeds have a deep sense of freedom, and this is one of their greatest desires. They are confident and secure in who they are and what they do. As a result, they are often happy to express themselves and try new things. They believe in equality of spirit and are highly intolerant of those who abuse their power or seek to dominate others. Because of this, Andromedans can often be perceived as rebellious, energetic, or temperamental.

- **You Feel a Very Strong Connection to Your Soul Group**

Once you realize that you are an Andromedan Starseed, you may be flooded with a feeling of belonging or even a sense of homecoming. This is because like attracts like, and the energy of Andromeda is something that your soul has been longing for its whole existence. Because of this connection, you can easily create a beautiful bond with other Andromedans.

Myth and Lore

Andromeda was the daughter of King Cepheus and Cassiopeia of Aethiopia. Cassiopeia, her mother, boasted that she was more beautiful than the Nereids, the handmaidens of the sea goddess Thetis. Angered by this insult, Poseidon sent a sea monster to ravage Aethiopia as divine punishment. Andromeda's parents were powerless against this attack, so they went to their Oracle for advice. The Oracle suggested that the King and Queen offer their daughter as a sacrifice to the monster, and without any consideration, Andromeda was chained to a rock on the shore, where she waited for death.

According to legend, Perseus was in the area on his way back from having slain Medusa and rescuing Andromeda's intended husband, Phineus, who had been turned into stone by Medusa's gaze. When he came upon Andromeda chained to a rock, Perseus immediately fell in love with her. He killed the monster with his sword, although some accounts claim that he used Medusa's head to turn the monster to stone. Either way, Andromeda was saved.

After her rescue, the goddess Athena promised Andromeda a place in the heavens, and when she died, the promise was fulfilled. Andromeda was given a place in the sky between the constellations of Cassiopeia, Cepheus, and Perseus. That place is known today as the Andromeda constellation, and the story of the beautiful princess and her heroic rescuer has been immortalized in the stars.

Finding Your Starseed Markings

Starseed markings are not birthmarks, as many might think, but something more intriguing. These markings are indicators on your natal chart that you may be a Starseed and can help you figure out which star system your soul originates from. Your natal chart holds a lot of insight into your life purpose and into your personality. It is based on the position of the planets when you were born, and it gives an energetic blueprint for your life. You can look at this energetic pattern and see what kind of experiences you'll have, what qualities you'll share with others, and what life lessons you'll learn. Each star-origin constellation has a pattern of energy that can be seen in the birth charts of all those born under that star origin. These markings are similar to fingerprints in that they are unique to each Starseed group and can be used as a way to identify who you truly are. This is because the natal chart reflects where we were before and where we are headed in this lifetime. It is a map of where we have been and a glimpse of what we can expect to experience as we move forward in our journey here on Earth.

The natal chart is not only for Starseeds; if you think you are a Starseed, you can get a chart reading from a professional astrologer familiar with star origins. The markings in your chart will be interpreted in the context of your genetic lineage, and the chart will be thoroughly analyzed to determine what traits and gifts you share with your star family. You can also look at your natal chart yourself, although it is recommended that you get a professional reading as this can be quite complex.

A Message for the Andromedan Starseed

Dear Andromedan, Starseed, you are one of the most glorious star families in the universe, and the DNA pattern that you carry within your body is only present in a few other Starseed groups. Although it may feel like you do not belong here, you do, and you have come to Earth at this time to help save this civilization from destroying itself. You are here to help raise human consciousness and support those ready to embrace their spiritual essence. You were born with a strong sense of innate knowing about your purpose, which is why you often feel driven or compelled by an intuitive guidance system. This makes it easy for you to find useful information about yourself or others.

The Andromedan Starseed is a highly intelligent being who has a deep sense of freedom and does not care to be told what to do. You enjoy learning about new things and visiting new places to experience different cultures, beliefs, and traditions. This makes you an excellent ambassador for your star family. You are here to teach and share the Andromedan teachings about love, truth, and unity with others. You have a deep sense of compassion for all living beings, and you'll do what is necessary to help others.

Chapter 5: Pleiadian Starseeds

Pleiadians are a race of beings from the Pleiades star system, approximately 430 light years from Earth. One of the nearest star systems to us, this beautiful cluster of stars, is located in the constellation Taurus and is easily visible to the naked eye. The Pleiades contains over 1,000 stars, although only a handful are easily visible. These stars are relatively young, estimated at around 100 million years. The brightest star in the cluster is Alcyone, which is around 10 times more massive than our Sun and around 10,000 times brighter.

Many ancient civilizations saw these stars as the Seven Sisters, and the name Pleiades comes from the Greek word "plein," meaning "to sail" or "to sail away." It is thought that they were regarded as the stars that would guide sailors safely to port, and the cluster was immortalized in the myth of the Seven Sisters, siblings who were transformed into these stars. These days, however, it is generally accepted that only six stars are visible to the naked eye, but some people have reported seeing seven stars in the Pleiades, and this has given rise to a legend that claims that one of the "missing" stars was banished to Earth for being too beautiful.

The Pleiades star system – believed to be the root of the Pleiadian Starseeds.[5]

Pleiadian Starseeds

Like other Starseeds, many Pleiadians have come here on Earth to help raise our consciousness as we transition from a 3rd-dimensional planet to a 4th-dimensional one. They come to assist us in our evolutionary journey as we progress toward becoming more spiritually and emotionally evolved beings, along with being more physically healthy. The Pleiadians have been here on Earth for many thousands of years, helping guide humanity through many great historical and cultural events. They are deeply connected to the history of our planet, and we have long shared a deep connection with them. They come from the 5th dimension and live as physical beings on Earth while maintaining awareness of their galactic connections. They are like us but have evolved to live without war, hunger, or greed.

On Earth, they live to help others find their way home and have been coming in ever-increasing numbers since 1987. They share their love of life with us and celebrate life on earth as a sacred gift from the Creator.

The Pleiadian Starseeds come into this life with a special cosmic purpose. They share their gifts and healing energy with us to help us awaken from our limited consciousness and limited perception of reality. Their mission is to bring us love, help us remember who we are, and reconnect us to our galactic heritage and divine nature. They are here to help break down the old system so we can experience the new.

For ALL extraterrestrial souls, Pleiades is known to be a focal point or school of learning. This "school" is unlike anything we can imagine; it is said to awaken extraordinary nurturing abilities, resolve imbalances between feminine and masculine energy, and sharpen creative energy. It is a place of learning that, paradoxically, does not involve the intellectual mind but rather the intuitive mind.

Our extraterrestrial allies find themselves in a state of constant wonderment at the sheer scope and depth of life on Earth. They experience reverence for the life forms they encounter and often find themselves awed by our planet's ability to thrive despite all of its obstacles. They are curious about our planet's history, culture, and religion, but until now, they have stayed out of the way of these conflicts and have refrained from interfering in our affairs. They have remained silent while we fought among ourselves for resources, power, land, and greed. They have watched the atrocities our planet has endured, and while they are sympathetic to our pain, they know we must learn from these experiences so that we may evolve as a race. It is now time for them to step forward and share their messages of love, hope, and freedom with us.

Characteristics of a Pleiadian Starseed

Pleiadians are often called the "keepers of knowledge," and their mission on Earth is to help humanity find its way back to its galactic family. They come from a higher spiritual plane where there is no war, poverty, or famine. The Pleiadians are here to help us remember who we really are and to reconnect us to our divine nature. They wish for us to reclaim our galactic heritage and remember that we are part of a greater family of star nations. Our extraterrestrial friends are here not only to share their knowledge with us but also to assist in elevating the vibration of the planet as a whole, so if you are a Pleiadian Starseed, the following traits will resonate with you:

1. Pleiadian Starseeds are sensitive individuals who are very empathic and feel things easily. Thinking of others before themselves, they have difficulty saying no when asked for help. They feel the suffering of others in their hearts and may become deeply involved in humanitarian causes if there is no one else to help. Because of their compassionate nature, they can experience depression if the reality surrounding them is too dark or painful.

2. Pleiadian Starseeds have a high level of keen intuitive perception that enables them to view the world uniquely. They understand that life is not just physical and that one should keep their mind and heart open to new possibilities.

3. Pleiadians are very spiritual beings, but they do not believe in religion. If you have studied religion, you may come to the conclusion that a large number of religions are missing the point. Religion is often used to control people and keep them from trusting their innate spirituality. Pleiadian Starseeds have no problem viewing God or the divine as a natural, beautiful entity akin to nature.

4. Pleiadians believe we are all part of a unit—one body with many different parts. Just like we have different organs, each with its own special function, our planet is also connected in this way. They understand that our connection to nature opens doors for us to communicate with it and ask for its assistance when we need healing or protection. They believe we are all one, connected to everything on the planet, and that we must come together as one super-galactic soul group to experience our true power.

5. Pleiadian Starseeds are musically inclined. They enjoy performing and listening to music because it opens them up to higher states of consciousness. Music can lead to feelings of bliss and ecstasy, which can be healing in itself.

6. Pleiadians like art for the same reason. It is an expression of the soul, something you feel instead of just seeing with your eyes. Like the songs they listen to, they find art profoundly moving and liberating. They love the idea that art is a language of communication available to all of us and can be used to heal and unite us.

7. Pleiadians are peaceful beings who can step aside from the issues of this planet and simply observe it from a higher place of understanding. They can often see that there is another way to approach our difficulties without getting involved in war or violence. They can make decisions that reflect their wisdom rather than following the narrow path of violence because it feels like the only way.

8. Pleiadians tend to be people-pleasers. Because they have compassion and understanding for others, they will go out of

their way to please the people around them. They can see where we are coming from, even when we do not see it ourselves. This sometimes leads them to be taken advantage of by others who may take their kindness for granted.
9. Pleiadians make excellent conversation partners because of their love of sharing ideas. They are often perceived as social butterflies because of their vibrant, outgoing personalities and a deep curiosity about the people around them.
10. Pleiadian Starseeds tend to be water signs, i.e., Pisces, Scorpio, and Cancer. Water signs have a deep psychic intuition that enables them to sense the emotions of others. These signs are also sensitive, imaginative, and highly attuned to their inner world. A water sign personality is an excellent match for a patriarchal society that places too much emphasis on materialism.

Myth and Lore

The Greek mythological account of the Pleiades is a favorite tale of the ancient Greeks. The Pleiades were the seven daughters of Atlas and Pleione and were known for their beauty and grace. However, their beauty caught the attention of Orion, a giant hunter who relentlessly pursued them. To protect the sisters from Orion's advances, Zeus transformed them into stars and placed them in the sky as a constellation. Today, the Pleiades are still fascinating for astronomers and stargazers alike. Their bright blue glow and distinctive pattern make them easy to spot in the night sky, and scientists have studied them extensively for decades. In addition to providing valuable scientific data, the Pleiades also hold cultural significance in many societies around the world. From ancient Greece to modern-day Japan, these seven stars continue to capture our imaginations and inspire us with their beauty and mystery.

A Message for the Pleiadian Starseed

Dear Pleiadian Starseed, your mission on Earth now is to be a part of the new spiritual, metaphysical, and scientific communities that are actively working to create a new paradigm of thinking based on unity consciousness and the understanding that we are all one. You have a strong telepathic connection to the Pleiades star cluster, and many of you may already be aware of your Starseed origins, though you may be confused about what that means right now. You have a deep desire to help the Earth and its inhabitants, and you want to find a way to make your life count for something meaningful. If this mission resonates with you, it is time to start thinking of ways to become more involved in humanitarian efforts and connect with others who are also seeking a greater purpose. Getting involved in new-age and spiritual communities is a great place to start.

Chapter 6: Sirian Starseeds

Sirius is a star in the Canis Major constellation and the brightest one in the night sky. It's also one of the closest stars to us, which is why scientists have heavily studied it. It is an ancient constellation representing a dog or hunting dog, particularly a large scent hound kept by royalty because of its speed and agility. Since the beginning of time, it has been a significant star. It was valuable to navigators who used it to measure distances in the night sky because it tended to brighten and then fade, allowing mariners to accurately fix their location. When making long journeys and voyages by sea, having a reference point to guide you on your path is always helpful.

The name Sirius comes from the Greek word "*seirios,*" which means scorching or fiery. It's a binary star system, meaning it has two stars: Sirius A and Sirius B. Sirius A is the brighter of the two, with Sirius B orbiting it. Ancient peoples believed that Sirius was a house or home for little dog-like beings, and many Native American tribes have stories about them. They knew that Sirius was a very important part of their existence because it could always be seen in the sky, and its movement helped them tell time, seasons, and even the status of their hunts. It also signified that life was possible on other worlds, specifically, that a star or planet might have life on it.

The origin of the Sirian Starseeds, known as Sirius.⁶

Sirian Starseeds

Sirian Starseeds have been coming to the planet Earth for a long time. These beings are often travelers, explorers, and math, science, and technology experts. They have a unique commitment to the advancement of knowledge and space exploration. They have dedicated their lives to truth, spiritual growth, and protecting life. They come to Earth as scientists, astronauts, inventors, philosophers, and spiritual teachers. They are patient, quiet, and love to read. They're free spirits who have a great sense of humor and like to joke around. They are also long-lived, highly intelligent, energetic, yet peaceful beings. Sirians are known for their contributions to the worlds of science, technology, and medicine. They discover cures, inventions, and vaccines for devastating diseases that have ravaged humankind in the past.

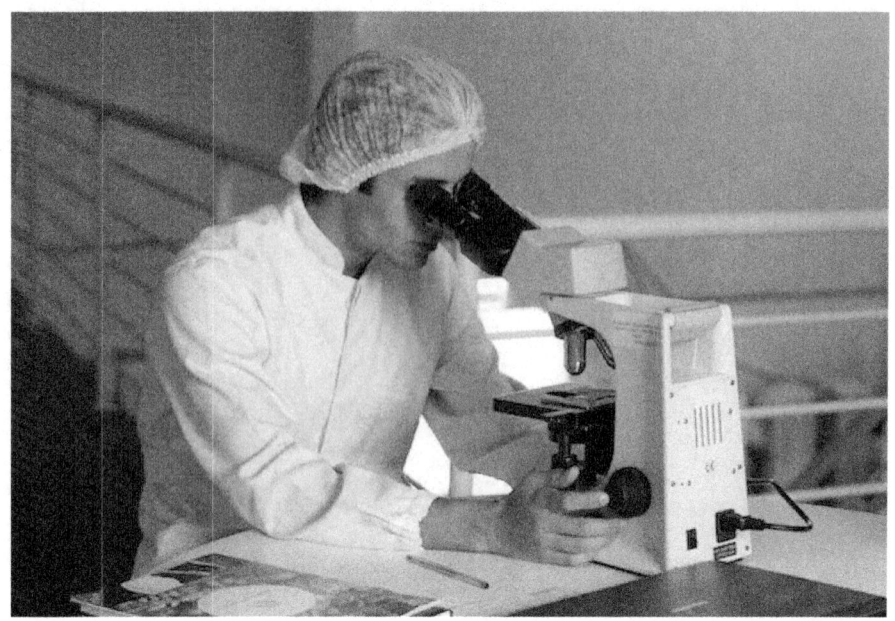
Sirian Starseeds love to benefit our Earth in any way they can.[7]

Sirians are attracted to people of all races and cultures. They tend to marry outside their race or nationality as they feel a strong sense of curiosity about other cultures and experiences. They also have a universal perspective on life, showing great respect for other races, cultures, and ethnicities. They're open and accepting of all people and value diversity.

These Starseeds typically have a highly developed spirituality and are conscious of their connection to the Earth. They respect nature and maintain a healthy balance between themselves and the world around them. They work diligently to maintain harmony between their surroundings, the environment, and other races. *They are such kind souls;* they are always willing to help others in need, making them natural caregivers. They feel a strong sense of compassion for others and want to heal the world. However, they should be careful about getting involved in everyone else's problems because they could end up neglecting themselves in the process.

Sirian Starseeds are fantastic therapists, teachers, and mentors for children. They're very thoughtful and insightful, and they love to be around children because they're so easy to connect with. These Starseeds can also be very intuitive and can be drawn to careers in the metaphysical or psychic fields. Known for their impeccable control over their emotions, they can make rational decisions when facing difficult situations. They are also highly empathetic and possess an in-depth knowledge of people's intentions, allowing them to predict outcomes and determine if others are being honest with them.

Their creativity and logic are legendary, making them good at solving problems and organizing events. However, they have a temper that makes them take everything personally. So, when something goes wrong, they assume it's their fault and turn their frustration inward.

Characteristics of a Sirian Starseed

1. **Great Sense of Humor:** Sirians love to joke around and make people laugh. They're witty and funny, and they enjoy playing practical jokes on their friends. They love to tell stories and have a great memory for humorous tales, which they don't mind sharing with others.
2. **Deep Thinker:** Sirians are quite analytical and enjoy discussing philosophical or metaphysical ideas with others. They can calm themselves by sitting in silent meditation, allowing their minds to drift away from stress-inducing situations.
3. **High IQ and Discipline:** Sirians love to work hard and stay focused, which makes them excellent students. They are also naturally organized and have a good head for math and science. They excel at problem-solving and logic and are always willing to learn new things.
4. **Strong Intuition:** Sirians have an innate sense of knowing what's happening around them and understand why people act in certain ways. This helps them get involved in the lives of others very easily, as they can relate to others on a deep level.
5. **Good Listeners:** Sirians don't always like to talk because they prefer to listen to others. They are very understanding and try not to judge people. This makes them great listeners, which others open up to quite easily.
6. **Love of Nature:** Sirians are passionate about the environment and try their best to do their part in preserving it. They respect nature and understand its importance in their lives.
7. **Laid-Back:** Sirians don't like to get stressed out or upset over things that they can't control. They tend to make compromises so everyone can enjoy the same level of happiness.

8. **Original Thinker:** Sirians have a good mind for problem-solving and are good at developing new ideas. This makes them extremely creative and innovative in whatever field they find themselves in.
9. **Natural Parent:** Sirians love kids; there's no other way to put it. They have a lot of patience to deal with them and are happy to help out friends with children.

Sirius and the Dogon Tribe

The Dogon Tribe is a group of indigenous people who live in Mali, in Western Africa; they are believed to be the ancestors of the Berbers. The Sirians visited them thousands of years ago, teaching them about astronomy, star worship, and reincarnation. The tribe identified Sirius as the home of beings, or star people, as they called them, who traveled across space in a blue lightship. These wise teachers gave them advanced knowledge of math, science, and medicine. They were responsible for creating the tribe's artwork, carvings, and statues. These star people even helped them build a massive, multistory structure called the granary. It was built on a large scale and was the only one of its kind in the entire region. They were also responsible for creating the tribe's hieroglyphic writings to store their advanced knowledge and wisdom.

Sirius and the Egyptians

Egyptian mythology had many connections to Sirius, and it was often referred to as Sothis. Not much is known about their early connection with the star, but it's suspected that they may have named the star after one of their gods. This would make sense, considering they were spiritual and deeply connected to their beliefs. It's also believed that Sirius may have been an important part of their culture because so many of their symbols are connected to it, including the eye, which represented divinity. They also considered the star a calendar and used it to guide them through the yearly life cycle and seasons. Sirius must have been especially crucial to their religion because the Egyptians claimed it was a portal connecting them to other worlds.

A Message to Sirian Starseeds

Dear Sirian, Starseed, you are called "Sun-seed" because you are the bearers of light and truth and are crucial to humanity as the Aquarius age begins. You contain the wisdom of all ages, and the bloodline from which you have come is significant. The akashic record is stored in the soul, and the physical form is the manifestation of the akashic record. This is why your work as a Starseed depends so much on your bloodline. Investigate your human ancestors to better understand the role you are to play in enhancing this particular bloodline. You are here to upgrade it and to increase spiritual awareness throughout the entire human race.

Your magnetic energy naturally inspires and uplifts others. You are here to guide people toward a higher truth and assist them in reconnecting with their true selves. Your dedication to spiritual work and developing your personal relationships is a priority for you. You are here on Earth to create harmony by bringing people together and creating unique solutions to problems.

You are a direct descendant of the Sirian race, which came to Terra approximately 250,000 years ago, along with the Lyrans. Although there have been many conflicts in this sector of the galaxy and in your own personal lives, you are here to help others resolve emotional and physical imbalances. Your destiny is to assist in the healing process as people awaken to their true spiritual heritage. Your ability to accurately read people and situations is what gives you your magic. Although you may possess many other spiritual gifts, this one stands out.

You are the Sirian Starseed. You are the one who struggles against your own personal limitations. You carry within you the gifts of your ancestors. Deep within you sleeps a mystical power that is awakening in this time of turmoil and chaos, a power that is waiting for the right time to be used to help humanity. Your path has been difficult, but it has led you to where you are today. Yours is the mission of making all things possible. This is your gift and your destiny.

Chapter 7: Lyran Starseeds

Lyra is a constellation of six officially named stars in the Northern celestial hemisphere. It's the smallest of all 88 constellations, but it's packed with interesting features and curious objects. Lyra is dominated by the bluish star Vega, one of the brightest stars in the night sky, with a magnitude of 0.03. Vega is also known for its fast rotation, which causes it to bulge at the equator and flatten at the poles. This unique feature has made it a popular subject of study for astronomers.

Aside from Vega, Lyra also contains several notable deep-sky objects, including the Ring Nebula, a planetary nebula formed when a star similar to our Sun ran out of fuel and shed its outer layers. Another interesting object in Lyra is the Beta Lyrae binary star system, which contains two stars so close together that they appear as one star to the naked eye. The two stars are so close that they revolve around a common center of mass, making them both orbit in the same plane and causing the pair to create a beautiful double image in binoculars. The Double-Double is another double star in Lyra that is visible in binoculars. It lies on the edge of the constellation, and the two stars take about 23 years to revolve around their common center of mass. The two stars are also only one magnitude apart, making them difficult to see together with the naked eye.

Lyran Starseeds are known for their great wisdom and psychic abilities.[8]

Lyra has been recognized by many cultures throughout history, including the Greeks, who associated it with the mythological figure Orpheus. In Chinese astronomy, Lyra is part of a larger constellation known as the Celestial Bird, and the image of a lyre, a harp-shaped instrument, was once used in the earliest Chinese star maps. Lyra may be small in size, but it's certainly not lacking in intrigue or significance. Its unique features and rich history make it an important area of study for astronomers and spiritualists alike.

Lyran Starseeds

The Lyran Starseeds, highly intelligent, evolved beings from Vega, the brightest planet in the Lyra constellation, are known as the original keepers of ancient knowledge and wisdom. They possess a deep understanding of the universe and its mysteries and are said to have played a key role in the development of human civilization on Earth. The Lyrans are believed to be one of the most ancient Starseed groups, with their origins dating back billions of years. The ancient Lyran civilization is compared to Earth's prehistoric "Romans" or "Egyptians" in the galaxy, and it is unlikely that first-generation Lyrans still exist.

The Lyrans are known throughout the galaxy for their presence in our solar system, and it is said that they first arrived on Earth approximately 4.3 billion years ago. They interacted with some of our earliest civilizations to influence their development here on Earth and appeared as "gods" to those early civilizations, helping teach them about the natural sciences and mystical arts, including astronomy, astrology, alchemy, and so on.

The Lyrans are described as spiritually advanced yet intellectually grounded beings who serve as a support system for other Starseeds. Their focus is on the expansion of consciousness and knowledge, particularly spiritual knowledge and wisdom that's beyond the grasp of normal human consciousness.

The Lyrans work with other Starseeds and assist them as they evolve their consciousness, imparting their wisdom and guidance where they are needed most. The Lyrans are said to have especially interacted with the Lemurians, considered to be humankind's early ancestors on Earth. These ancient beings are also closely tied to the Vegan Starseeds, who some believe to be their offspring.

Unlike other Starseeds, which are often associated with one particular star in a constellation, the Lyrans have their origins among the planets and stars of the Lyra constellation. This means that most Lyran Starseeds don't have a home planet to call their own. Instead, they form communities or nomadic groups to live on different planets while traveling back and forth between them and Vega.

Lyran Starseeds are said to possess high levels of psychic and creative abilities, which are believed to be amplified while traveling and living among other Starseed groups. They are also believed to have certain powers allowing them to heal their emotional and physical bodies. With this ability, they can work with a person's chakras, bringing them back into alignment by opening up blocked energy centers and facilitating energy flow through them.

Characteristics of a Lyran Starseed

Lyran Starseeds have several qualities that make them stand out from other Starseeds. The following are some of the traits that these Starseeds may experience or display throughout their lives:

- **You Feel Like an Old Soul:** Lyran Starseeds often have a deep sense of wisdom and understanding beyond their years. You may feel like you have been on this earth for a long time, even if you are relatively young. This is because Lyrans have a strong connection to their past lives and ancestral lineage, which gives them a sense of grounding and stability in this lifetime.

- **You Love Adventure:** You have a great sense of adventure that can take you to interesting places. You really love the thrill of discovery and enjoy going to new and exotic places.

- **You Are an Enthusiastic Traveler:** You love traveling in other realms just as much as you enjoy exploring the physical world, so you are drawn to astral projection, lucid dreaming, and out-of-body experiences. These activities allow you to broaden your perspective and see things from different points of view. By observing these alternative realities through different lenses, you can learn a lot about yourself and our world.

- **You Are Drawn to History and Historical Events:** You are also fascinated by ancient knowledge from civilizations throughout the ages. You want to explore the mysteries and secrets of the past to learn how to better understand the present and future.

- **You Tend to Go with the Flow of Life:** Lyran Starseeds have a deep sense of trust in the universe and its plan for them. They don't resist change or try to control outcomes but instead allow life to unfold naturally. This doesn't mean they're passive or lack ambition, but rather that they're open to new experiences and opportunities that come their way.

- **You Easily Manifest Your Reality:** Lyran Starseeds possess a powerful ability to effortlessly manifest their desires. They understand that their thoughts and emotions directly impact their reality and use this knowledge to create the life they want. They don't struggle or fight to make things happen but instead trust that the universe will bring them what they need at the right time.

- **You Are Not the Most Patient:** While Lyran Starseeds have a strong sense of trust in the universe, they can sometimes struggle with patience. They have a deep desire to see their dreams come to fruition quickly and may become frustrated when things don't happen as fast as they would like. However, they understand that everything happens in divine timing and that their impatience can actually block the flow of abundance. As such, they work on cultivating patience and surrendering to the natural flow of life.

- **You Value Authenticity:** Lyran Starseeds place a high value on authenticity and genuineness. They believe being true to oneself is essential for personal growth and spiritual evolution. They are not interested in putting on a façade or pretending to be someone they are not, as they know that this only hinders their progress. Instead, they strive to be honest and transparent in all their interactions with themselves and others. This commitment to authenticity allows them to form deep and meaningful connections with those around them and the universe itself.

- **You Are Fascinated by the Magical Arts:** You are endlessly curious about the intricate rituals, the ancient symbols, and the mystical energies surrounding us. You spend countless hours studying and practicing various forms of divination, from tarot readings to crystal scrying. Your intuition is finely tuned, and you trust your inner guidance to lead you on your spiritual path. You seek out like-minded individuals who share your passion for the occult, and together, you explore the mysteries of the universe. You have gained a deeper understanding of yourself and the world around you through dedication to the magical arts. You know there is much more to life than meets the eye, and you constantly seek new ways to connect with the divine. Your journey is one of self-discovery and enlightenment, and you embrace it with open arms.

Myth and Lore

The story of the Lyra constellation begins with the Greek mythological figure of Orpheus. Orpheus was the son of Apollo, the god of music and prophecy, and Calliope, one of the Muses. He was a skilled musician and poet who played songs that could move even rocks to tears. He had a wife named Eurydice, who died from a snake bite, and in an act of grief, he ventured into the underworld to bring her back to life. Hoping that music would soothe Hades' heart, Orpheus played such sad songs that Hades wept for him. Touched by Orpheus' music, Hades allowed Eurydice to return to the land of the living with one condition—Orpheus could not look back at her until they had left the underworld.

However, when he finally reached the surface and opened his eyes, he realized that she wasn't behind him. In his haste to get her, he disobeyed the rule of Hades and looked back before she reached safety. As a result, Eurydice disappeared back into the underworld forever.

Orpheus was devastated and spent the rest of his life mourning her loss. He wandered the earth, playing mournful tunes on his lyre, hoping to find solace in his music. His songs were so sorrowful that even the animals and trees would weep when they heard him play. Eventually, his grief became too much to bear, and he decided to join Eurydice in the underworld. He descended into Hades' realm again, but this time he was not allowed to leave. His tragic story moved the gods, and they placed his lyre in the sky as a constellation so that his music could continue to be heard for eternity. And so, Orpheus' legacy lived on through his music, a testament to the power of love and the pain of loss.

A Message for the Lyran Starseed

Dear Lyran Starseed, you are not alone in this universe. Your soul comes from the Lyra constellation, a place of great spiritual power and wisdom. You have been sent to Earth to share your unique gifts and help raise the collective consciousness of humanity. Your mission is not easy, but it is filled with purpose and meaning.

Like Orpheus, you have a special connection to music and the arts. Your creative talents are a powerful tool for healing and transformation. Use them wisely and with intention, for they can touch people's hearts in ways that words cannot. But remember, your journey on Earth is not without its challenges. The pain of loss may be something you are familiar with, but it can also teach you great lessons about the nature of love and the human experience.

As you navigate this life, know that your spirit guides and higher self are always with you, offering guidance and support along the way. They have watched over you since the beginning of time and will continue to offer you strength and guidance in your life's journey.

Don't be afraid to reach out for help when you need it, for many people can help you on your path. And know that the journey is not over until it is complete. Follow your spirit and keep moving forward, for this is how you'll find your way home again, to the stars from whence you came.

Chapter 8: Orion Starseeds

Orion is a wonderful constellation for stargazers and people who just want to bask in the glory of nature's wonderment. The physical body of this constellation is visible from anywhere on Earth (except Antarctica), so it's easy to find with some simple calculations and by looking through a telescope or binoculars. Three stars in this constellation form a bright and easily recognizable belt. Alnitak is the highest of the three but not the brightest. Alnilam is slightly lower and is a supergiant star, the brightest in the belt. It has about 374,000 times the Sun's luminosity and is 1,300 light years away from Earth. Mintaka is on a lower level than Alnilam and is actually a binary star system, which means that there is a smaller companion star orbiting it. This celestial pattern was first observed by the ancient Greeks and was said to represent a hunter's belt.

Orion Starseeds have guided humanity through evolutionary stages and still are.[9]

On the other hand, Orion's three belt stars aren't the only bright stars in the constellation. There are actually a total of seven bright stars in Orion: Alnitak, Alnilam, Mintaka, Betelgeuse (which is Orion's right shoulder), Bellatrix (his left shoulder), Saiph (his right knee), and Rigel (his foot). The brightest of these stars is Rigel, a blue-white supergiant and the 8th brightest star in the night sky.

Several deep-sky objects in Orion may also interest stargazers and amateur astronomers. The Great Orion Nebula is one of the brightest diffuse nebulae in the sky. It's so bright that it can be seen with the naked eye from a dark site without binoculars or a telescope. It is believed to be an interstellar cloud of gas and dust, a wonderful home to many new stars being born and many old stars dying.

Orion Starseeds

The Orion Starseeds are a race of benevolent explorers who have been guiding Earth's evolution for millennia. They represent an advanced society that has mastered space travel and other galactic technologies. Choosing to become the caretakers of our planet, they have been with us during our most important evolutionary stages. The last ice age is a good example. They were present behind the scenes, helping to facilitate our species' survival by providing us with technology and watching for the most advantageous times to influence particular events.

It has been speculated that beings from Orion created Atlantis and Lemuria, during which time they taught us how to use crystals and heal ourselves. They were also involved in mankind's move from Lemuria to Atlantis and the beginning of this civilization. They then helped us with the move from Atlantis to Egypt, where they taught us hieroglyphics, mathematics, and advanced agriculture.

Over many thousands of years, the Orions have guided us through times of great change. They are among the few star races with an affinity with Earth, which resonates with their personal experiences here. It's been said that they have spent thousands of years in various incarnations on Earth, from giants to humans, and their influence is still present in many places on Earth today through their artifacts buried in the soil or secret chambers hidden deep beneath oceans and ancient mountains.

Orion Starseeds are known for their compassion, generosity, and love of human beings. They are very aware of the value of life and work hard to keep life-giving systems healthy. They also have an inherent need to study humanity as a species to better understand our nature and what we need.

They believe in continuous learning and will always seek out opportunities for growth and personal development. They are very much into the whole concept of evolution and will often be found observing other planets through telescopes or other forms of remote sensing. Some can astrally travel through the stars as well as space, which allows them to easily move from planet to planet, star system to star system, or galaxy to galaxy.

Characteristics of an Orion Starseed

- **You Can Be Accurately Described as Curious:** Orion Starseeds are very concerned about education and will always try to learn as much as possible. They are very inquisitive about the nature of the universe and seek to understand how it all works. They always want to know how things evolve from one state to another and why they take a particular path.

- **You Are Extremely Creative:** The Orion Starseeds are extremely capable of coming up with ideas that can help solve problems. They are very good problem solvers and excel at putting things together in a way that never existed before. They have an innovative mind that beautifully combines existing information and skills to create something unique and untested.

- **You Are Vigilant, Attentive, and Insightful:** The Orion Starseeds are always aware of their surroundings and will not allow anything to happen without their knowledge or approval. They will be the first to notice anything that is out of the ordinary and are always on the verge of discovering, ready to make sense of new things they encounter. They try to anticipate what is going to happen and have a plan for how to act accordingly.

- **You Take Your Duties Very Seriously:** This is one of the most important characteristics found in Orion Starseeds. They know what is right and what is wrong and won't allow themselves to get caught up in things that cause harm to others or themselves. They are very conscious of their destiny and will do everything possible to ensure their own well-being and that of other entities within their sphere of influence.

- **You Are Compassionate:** Orion Starseeds place a lot of importance on human life and will always try to help those in need. They would go out of their way to save someone from a burning building or stop a violent attack. They believe in supporting the less fortunate whenever possible and enjoy helping others when they can without needing to receive anything in return.

- **You Are Curious about Spirituality:** Orion Starseeds will always pursue spiritual enlightenment and answers to the mysteries of life. They want to understand their own existence and how they fit into the bigger picture. They will never be satisfied unless they know how everything fits together and why certain things happen.

- **You Love a Good Challenge:** Orion Starseeds enjoy being challenged. When they are presented with a situation that seems daunting to everyone else, they will jump on it. It allows them to sharpen their skills and apply their intelligence in ways that matter to them. They don't like the feeling of defeat and will apply whatever pressure it takes to ensure the desired outcome. They are natural-born athletes, explorers, and pioneers because they love the thrill of conquering a difficult task or goal. Once they have reached a certain milestone, they are not the type to just bask in that achievement; they want more.

- **You Are a Natural Leader:** Orion Starseeds can be found leading groups of people and have a natural way of inspiring those with whom they work alongside. They are very good at giving directions and finding ways to make them both efficient and creative at the same time. You'll find them at the frontlines, where everyone can see them, and they will give commands that the rest of the crowd will follow without question. They enjoy being in charge and will always take on a leadership role whenever possible.

- **You Are Opinionated:** Orion Starseeds have a strong sense of self and always follow their own intuition. They are not the type to shy away from raising their voice to make an important point or stand up for what they believe is right. They are very determined to get others to see the world as they do, and this can be very challenging for them when faced with people who oppose their belief system.

Myth and Lore

The earliest account of this tale describes Orion as the child of the god Poseidon and Euryale, princess of King Minos of Crete. One day, he set out determined to reach the island of Chios, and he succeeded because of his father, who gave him the ability to walk on water. Drunk out of his mind, he attempted to seduce Merope, the local king's daughter; as punishment, he was blinded and thrown off the island by King Oenopion. Blind Orion quickly made his way to Lemnos, the location of the forge that belonged to the god Hephaestus, and with the aid of the fire god, Orion made it to the East, where the sun god Helios healed his blindness.

With his sight restored, Orion continued his travels, eventually returning to Crete, where he met Princess Artemis. The two quickly fell in love and became inseparable. Together, they hunted and roamed the countryside, with Orion's skills as a hunter impressing even the goddess of the hunt herself. However, their happiness was short-lived as Apollo, Artemis' twin brother, became jealous of their relationship and tricked Artemis into killing Orion. Devastated by her actions, Artemis pleaded with Zeus to place Orion among the stars as a constellation. There, he could be forever remembered as the greatest hunter that ever lived.

A Message for the Orion Starseed

Dear Orion Starseed, it's time for you to open your eyes and see the world for what it truly is. Life has been a series of tests, but now you are ready to enter a whole new world that hasn't even begun to be explored yet by the rest of humanity. You have been chosen to face this huge task as a leader on behalf of your community. You were selected because you have courage and spiritual strength. It is your time to shine because everyone is waiting for you to step up and bring them into this brave new world you envisioned.

The time of ruling one another is at an end. It's time to create a society where spirituality is valued, and those who are the leaders on all levels of the hierarchy are in their positions because of their character and not because of their wealth or good looks. It's time for everyone to know the truth about how we got here and what our purpose really is as a species. You'll help humanity realize all these things, but you'll have to be patient and let things progress at the pace that they need to. It's been a long time coming, and things will happen as soon as they are ready. So, keep your head up and trust that the universe is on your side.

Chapter 9: Arcturian Starseeds

Arcturus is a red giant star located in the constellation of Boötes. It is one of the brightest stars in the night sky and is easily visible to the naked eye. It is around 37 light-years from Earth and is the brightest star in its constellation. The star's surface temperature is around 4,300 Kelvin, giving it its distinctive orange-red color, and it has a diameter approximately 25 times larger than that of our sun.

Despite being an old star, Arcturus still shines brightly due to its size and high luminosity. It is estimated to be around 7 billion years old, meaning it has already exhausted most of its hydrogen fuel and will eventually evolve into a white dwarf star. Despite being well-known as the brightest star in its constellation, another interesting fact about this red giant is that it is believed to be the home star of the Arcturian race, which includes many humanoid extraterrestrials.

The home star of the Arcturian Starseeds.[10]

Arcturian Starseeds

Arcturian Starseeds have incarnated on Earth from the Arcturus star system. In most cases, they don't realize they come from Arcturus until much later in life. They are often strongly interested in space, science, philosophy, metaphysics, and esoteric fields. They also have an interest in exploring the unknown, which could be how they got here in the first place over 120,000 years ago.

Arcturian Starseeds often feel like they don't belong on Earth and like they are only here for a reason. An Arcturian Starseed can experience bouts of depression or fatigue due to the extreme contrast between how they feel on the inside and how they appear to be on the outside. Some may feel trapped in their physical bodies and the third dimension, but when they awaken to their true nature, they will be able to see that this was a vehicle for their consciousness to explore and develop in.

According to Edgar Cayce, the existence of Arcturians is thought to take place in a dimension of clarity beyond human comprehension. Humans would find their planet's purity and clarity to be very energizing, and upon first contact with them, one would feel a personal purification. With the Arcturians, there would no longer be any need for the extra baggage we have in this third-dimensional world, and this world would be able to heal from its current state of disrepair.

Arcturians don't worry about things like physical survival, safety, retirement, pensions, or even simple forms of labor. These topics are outside of their purview. Instead, they give their time and energy to the spiritual life but do not mistake this for a life without pleasure. They also have relationships and enjoy music. They work as well, but not at the level of squalor required by our culture and society. Their work better fits their personal preferences and spiritual journeys.

Arcturians are also extremely peaceful people. They haven't fought in battle in a very long time. Yes, they are capable of appearing in the third dimension, and yes, they can defend themselves if need be, but they typically aren't involved in anything that even remotely resembles a conflict. It is said that they can instantly dematerialize if there is a problem. Any projectile that comes their way would simply pass through them without harming them. This is a skill that some other extraterrestrial civilizations have mastered.

Arcturians also experience the death of their form on Arcturus, but they do so in a very different way because it is only seen as a temporary phase of their existence, not as the end. When they incarnate on Earth, they'd rather spend their time enjoying the physical world and using it as a way to experience more diversity and clarity of consciousness. The idea of aging would be looked upon with a sense of humor. We can learn something from this and embrace the present because it is an opportunity to use the here and now as an arena for experiencing who we are.

Another thing of note is that Arcturians haven't been directly involved in the genetic or evolutionary changes that have occurred in human DNA. The Sirians and Pleiadians were left to handle those matters. Arcturians primarily served as supervisors or teachers, and now they are here to assist us in completing our cycle so that we can enter the stargate and ascend to the fifth dimension.

Characteristics of an Arcturian Starseed

- **You Are Highly Organized:** You like to be precise with time and life events. You are meticulous with your work schedule and appointments.

- **You Are Mostly Interested in Science and Technology:** You enjoy exploring the mysteries of life through technology, scientific experiments, space travel, computers, medicine, and alternative healing techniques. There is a tendency to be an over thinker, and you want to understand everything in depth.

- **You Are Very Mysterious:** Getting to know you is hard because you keep your personal life private. You are a solid friend and family member but are cautious when disclosing information about yourself. It is rare for you to get close to someone or open up too quickly.

- **You Love Your Space:** While you enjoy socializing with close friends and family, you often need alone time to recharge your batteries. You enjoy sitting by yourself and watching the stars. It's not uncommon for you to have a nagging feeling that you don't really belong here on Earth. It could be the crowds, cities, or intense environments.

- **You Have a Knack for Public Speaking:** You are good at giving speeches and expressing your ideas. You know how to get people to listen to you when you are passionate about a subject.

- **You Value Logic:** You tend to use your mind more than your heart when dealing with problems and making decisions. You can analyze situations objectively and come up with practical solutions. This will serve you well in business but not so well in relationships.
- **You Love Creating:** Despite your logical nature, you also have a creative side. You enjoy writing, drawing, or playing music in your spare time. It's one of the few ways you express yourself.
- **You Are Very Intuitive:** You feel that there is a greater truth in the universe that cannot be unraveled by reason alone. Your intuition is a great guide for you, but it can also cause you to feel lonely or isolated from other people at times because it is not something everyone understands or comprehends.
- **You Have an Incredible Eye for Detail:** You can easily become bored or frustrated if things don't have a certain degree of precision. You have a passion for accuracy and ensure everything is in its proper place, just like it should be. It's one reason you don't like to be around those who are not as organized and precise.

Myth and Lore

At least two Greek myths feature Arcturus. The first connects Arcas and Callisto's constellations, Boötes and Ursa Major. In this tale, Hera, the wife of Zeus, changed Callisto into a bear after learning of her husband's adultery. Callisto wandered the woods for a while before she ran into her grown-up son, Arcas. Arcas pulled his spear out of fear for the large bear in front of him. Zeus, however, stepped in right away to avert a catastrophe. Callisto and Arcas were taken up into the heavens by a whirlwind; Arcas was turned into Boötes, and Callisto became Ursa Major.

Arcturus is also linked to the legend of Icarius in another myth. Icarius, an Athenaean, received the gift of wine as a token of appreciation from the god Dionysus. He proceeded to give the wine to some shepherds he encountered, and they became drunk. Thinking Icarus had poisoned them, they killed him and left his body in the bushes. Erigone, Icarius' daughter, and Maera, her dog, soon came upon his body, and they were so distraught that they committed suicide.

Dionysus decided to punish the city of Athens with a plague because he was so furious. The plague finally ended after the Athenians instituted rituals to remember Icarius and Erigone. Icarius, Erigone, and Maera were transformed by Dionysus into the constellations Boötes, Virgo, and the star Procyon (Maera).

A Message for the Arcturian Starseed

Dear Arcturian Starseed, know that your unique perspective on the world is truly a gift. Your ability to see things precisely and clearly is a rare talent that should be celebrated. However, I also understand that this can sometimes make you feel isolated or misunderstood by others who may not share your level of awareness. You must remember that while your perception may differ, it doesn't make it any less valid or valuable. Embrace your individuality and continue to use your keen eye for detail to make positive changes in the world around you. But don't forget to stay open to new ideas and experiences. You must be willing to understand why people do the things they do if you hope to form positive relationships with them. You must learn to be flexible if you want to adapt to different circumstances as they arise.

You are here to do great things, and nothing will stand in your way. Paradoxically, the very thing you are most gifted at doing is also what will trip you up the most. Be careful that your critical eye does not become so focused on the things that need to be improved that it causes you to miss seeing the beauty in what already exists.

Don't let other people's reactions prevent you from doing what makes your heart happy or allowing yourself the freedom of experimentation. Your awareness is a gift that needs to be treated with respect and dignity. You must also learn to balance your need for personal space with your desire for close relationships. You already have a strong support network in place, and all you need to do is trust yourself enough to allow them into your life. Change is scary sometimes, but that's what makes it so exhilarating.

Chapter 10: Vega Starseeds

Vega is a star in the Lyra constellation that is known for its brightness and beauty. It is the fifth-brightest star in the sky and can be seen from almost anywhere on Earth. It is also a relatively young star, estimated to be only about 455 million years old. It has a mass roughly 2.1 times that of the sun and a radius about 2.7 times larger. Vega's temperature is also much hotter than the sun, with a surface temperature of around 9,600 Kelvin.

One of the most interesting things about Vega is its rapid rotation, which causes it to bulge at the equator and flatten at the poles. This phenomenon is known as oblateness and is a result of the centrifugal force generated by Vega's fast spin. In addition to that, Vega is classified as a blue-white star, meaning that it emits most of its light in the blue and ultraviolet parts of the spectrum, making it one of the brightest stars in the sky and an important target for astronomers studying stellar evolution.

In recent years, Vega has been found to have a debris disk—a ring of dust and debris orbiting around it—which could indicate collisions between asteroids or comets or the presence of exoplanets. The study of Vega's debris disk has provided valuable insights into the formation and evolution of planetary systems, as it is believed that such disks are the birthplace of planets. In fact, the presence of a debris disk around Vega suggests that there may be planets orbiting the star, although none have been detected yet, at least not scientifically. Scientists continue to study Vega and its surrounding environment to better understand the processes that shape our universe. As technology advances and new discoveries are made, we can expect to learn more about this fascinating star and its mysteries.

The Vega star, where the Vega Starseeds came from.[11]

Vega Starseeds

The brightest star system in the constellation of Lyra, Vega, is the origin of the alien species known as the Vega Starseed. They are also referred to as Vegans, and no, this has zero to do with the diet. Vegans came from Lyra so that they could colonize and rule Sirius, the dog star. They are said to be descendants of the oldest known humanoid species and are, without a doubt, the most advanced in this galaxy. Of course, they can also reincarnate on Earth, where they typically assume a humanoid form with gorgeous dark skin and raven hair. Some also come in subtle copper undertones, enhancing their ethereal beauty. Still, on their home planet, their skin is said to have a bluish tint.

The Vega Starseed has many characteristics of an enlightened being, but none is more important than loving unconditionally. This means that their love extends to all sentient beings, even those who do not meet their standards for behavior. When it comes to relationships, they are both empathetic and extremely seductive. They have huge hearts and are always willing to listen to the needs of others, but they will never allow themselves to be taken advantage of. Though they are extremely generous with their love and support, they do not make it a habit of allowing themselves to be used. If anyone ever tries to manipulate them into giving more than what is reasonable, they will show that person the door—no exceptions.

Vegans' amount of love has no limit.[12]

Many Vegans are kind, but that is not always the case. They are also known to be completely ruthless and unforgiving if anyone should betray them or cross them in any way. They are not above doing whatever it takes to exact revenge, and they will not think twice about doing so if warranted. These people are far more advanced than humans could ever imagine, and because of their exceptional talent and creativity, they have been able to settle on or colonize several planets in our galaxy. Regardless, they are a friendly species because they have empathy and are old souls who are extremely conscious of the universe's interconnectedness.

Characteristics of a Vega Starseed

- **Inconsistent Yet Creative:** They are extremely creative and intelligent but also very unpredictable. They often switch between having unconventional beliefs one day and acting far more conventionally the next.

- **Like to Live in Exotic Places:** Many Vega Starseeds go out of their way to visit different countries in search of that one place where they can feel at home. They are almost addicted to moving around and enjoy traveling to remote locations with breathtaking scenery.

- **Can Be Very Officious:** If you are working with a Vega Starseed, do not forget that they have their own ideas of what is acceptable and what is not. You may think you can boss them around, but your chances of success are slim. Their confidence in who they are will not allow them to be pressured into doing something just because someone else thinks it should be done a certain way.

- **Always Seeking to Learn More:** Vega Starseeds are always seeking to gather more information about themselves and the world around them. They keep an open mind and like to discuss and debate various ideas that they come across.

- **The Center of Attention:** Usually, these individuals are excellent conversationalists, which means that they can talk just about anyone into anything. This is a natural gift for them, but it also comes in handy when they try to tell you why you should do what they want you to do.

- **Are Not Afraid to Look into the Future:** Though many humans have this ability, Vega Starseeds are especially good at it because they have a natural knack for intuition. They love working with channels, tarot cards, and other forms of mediumship because it allows them to tap into their abilities even further.

- **Not Afraid to Let You Know What They Are Thinking:** Vega Starseeds are open about their feelings, and if you have them as a friend, they will be honest enough to tell you exactly what they think of you. This is both a blessing and a curse because they will not hesitate to tell you about it when things go wrong in the relationship.

- **Can Be Ruthless:** When betrayed, Vega Starseeds are known to easily turn on their former friends and close associates. They tend to cut people off without a second thought – and never look back.
- **Fiercely Loyal:** Vega Starseeds are protective of the ones they love and will go to great lengths to protect them from the harshness of this world. This can sometimes manifest as obsession, so they must learn to set healthy boundaries with their loved ones.

Myth and Lore

According to legend, Vega, a goddess of the heavens, and Altair, a human, were once lovers. Vega, the princess of the skies, felt very alone and isolated as she flew through the heavens. One day, she approached a handsome man she had seen sitting beneath a large tree to listen to the music he was playing on his flute. He was delighted and surprised to see her, and he immediately fell in love with her. In the days that followed, she paid him a visit every day because she had fallen in love with the Earthly cow herder. She promised that no matter what happened, they would be in the Heavens one day together.

In some versions of the story, her mother is the one who learns about the forbidden romance. It's her father in others. However, the outcome is the same: they drag Vega away and forbid her from seeing this mortal. A cruel turn of events sees the fulfillment of her promise, and the two lovers are placed in the skies, though they are far apart and will always be divided by the Heavens. With Vega in the constellation Lyra and Altair in the constellation Aquila, the Great Celestial River, which is the Milky Way, lay between them.

A bridge of magpies is said to form once a year on the seventh day of the seventh month of the traditional Chinese calendar, letting the lovers be together for a single day. However, it's not always feasible to meet. The legend claims that if it rains on this day, the lovers will not be able to see one another and that the rain is actually Vega's tears falling from the heavens.

The story of Vega and Altair gives people hope that, against all odds and despite the extreme distance, people who are connected at heart can still find each other, even if it takes a while. There is always a chance where there is great love.

A Message for the Vega Starseed

Dear Vega Starseed, you have done this a thousand times over in a thousand different lifetimes. You have had many names, but you are always the same person. You are a warrior, a protector, and a guardian of light. Your fierce loyalty is one of your greatest strengths but can also be your downfall if you do not learn to balance it with healthy boundaries. Remember that you cannot save everyone, and sometimes the best thing you can do is let go and trust that they will find their own way.

Your mission on this planet is to bring light and love to those who need it most. You are here to heal the wounds of the past and create a brighter future for all beings. But to do this, you must first heal yourself. Take time to connect with your inner self and listen to the whispers of your soul. Trust your intuition and follow your heart, even when it leads you down an unfamiliar path. You possess many gifts but are only as powerful as you choose to be.

Chapter 11: Maldekian Starseeds

This chapter is about a planet believed to have existed eons ago. The asteroid belt (which includes the dwarf planet Ceres) is thought to have formed as a result of Phaeton (or Maldek), a hypothetical planet that the Titius-Bode law hypothesized may have existed between Mars and Jupiter's orbits. The fictitious planet was named "*Phaeton*" in honor of Phaethon, a character from Greek mythology who attempted unsuccessfully for one day to drive his father's solar chariot before being slain by Zeus.

Phaeton is a fascinating concept that has captured the imagination of scientists and astronomers for centuries. While it remains a hypothetical planet scientifically, the idea of its existence has helped us better understand the formation of our solar system. The asteroid belt we know today is believed to be the remnants of Phaeton, which was destroyed in a catastrophic collision with another celestial body. It is believed that this

Maldekian Starseeds are mysterious and secretive except with their trusted ones.[13]

event may have also contributed to the formation of Jupiter's moons and even Earth. Even though many scientists have disregarded its existence, Phaeton has left an indelible mark on our understanding of the universe and serves as a reminder of the enigmas that still await us in space.

Maldekian Starseeds

All you have read so far is science's version of the story. Let's look at what mediums, spiritualists, and esotericism have to say about it. Trusted channelers have revealed that Phaeton, which was actually called *Maldek*, was run into the ground by invaders. Imagine the world in a thousand years with nuclear war, pollution, and survivors in underground bunkers believing they are safe from harm. This was Maldek at some point in their history. It was once a planet occupied by light beings with infinite wisdom and knowledge. There was even a time when angels used it as a base between incarnations and missions. Maldek was incredibly old, with some saying it existed before the Pleiades. The beings there were incredibly misunderstood but still gave unconditional love.

Their planet was invaded by a different race, which attempted to seize total control of the area, and the Maldekians engaged in a losing battle for survival. They shared the same technology but were too full of love to actually use it against the other group. As a result, Maldek exploded into pieces as the invaders dealt the final blow. While some souls could move onto higher dimensions, Maldek itself ceased to exist. Also breaking into tiny pieces was the consciousness of Maldekians, and according to channeled transmissions, there are many Maldekian souls with fragments of themselves dispersed throughout the cosmos.

That is too much agony to experience, and it's unlikely to go away in a few lifetimes. It travels with them. They tend to feel lost and would like to go home, but they never do because they are aware in the back of their minds that their home has already been lost. As Starseeds, they experience feelings of having a twin or being lost and cut off from the family they were born into. They've never had a sense of community. They have grieving souls and appear to be in pain, but they are never sure why. The source of their suffering is deeper than meets the eye, so they are usually given diagnoses for manic depression and anxiety disorders without any basis in fact.

Maldekian Starseeds typically gravitate toward archeology because they are looking for anything their kind left behind on this planet, as many came here after the catastrophe that befell their home. They would have settled in hot, dry areas like ancient Egypt or Mexico or areas with high altitudes such as the Andes, Alps, Rockies, and Himalayas. They would have been among the first alien populations to thrive on Earth because they were once highly advanced.

Maldekians are very sensitive to materialism, yet they still crave material things like art that is created with care and love. They don't need to read a book because they are inherently wise. They are easily bored here because they are already familiar with everything. They are obstinate and strong-willed and prefer to observe others while remaining inconspicuous. Although they usually try to keep a low profile to avoid missing anything, they are quite sociable. However, they lack relationships and are very untrusting. They don't often get married, but when they do, they mate for life.

They have a crude sense of humor that borders on slapstick, especially when acting extremely silly for amusement. These souls will laugh at anything because laughter, as people say, is the best medicine. It makes them feel better, and it will also make people around them laugh.

Their physical appearance is usually striking. They are beautiful and fascinating but very mysterious at the same time. Maldekian Starseeds always appear very old and wise, with a haunted look in their eyes. Despite their good nature and willingness to go above and beyond for others, they have a darker side. They are well-liked by others but dislike others. Despite being a loner, they appear well-known and friendly around other people. However, only those who share their values can see their true colors because they are secretive and refuse to let others in. They are excellent at lying, not because they are dishonest people but as a coping mechanism that prevents them from telling others what they really think or how they truly feel.

Characteristics of a Maldekian Starseed

- They are sensitive and have a deep longing to feel safe.
- They might appear very wise but have an inquisitive nature that can border on insubordination.
- They could also appear withdrawn and lonely, but they are very sociable with their own kind.

- In stressful situations, they will react violently or verbally aggressively towards those around them because they feel threatened in some way by this person, people, or situation.
- They can be very rebellious, stubborn, or unyielding.
- They could appear to be self-centered and selfish when, in reality, they're just trying to protect themselves from others' criticism, as they are overly sensitive and easily hurt.
- They are drawn to fire and bright light.
- Their lives tend to be uneventful and boring because they are not interested in action or adventure.

Myth and Lore

The child of Helios, the sun god, and Clymene, a mortal, Phaethon resided with his mother due to his father's challenging task. Helios was in charge of driving the Sun's chariot across the Earth during the day, which resulted in the sun rising and setting.

One day, a classmate of Phaethon's made fun of him for saying he was the god's son and stated he didn't believe him. In sorrow, Phaethon requested proof of his paternity from his mother. After reassuring him that he was, in fact, the son of the mighty god Helios, Clymene sent her son to his father's palace to demonstrate his legitimacy.

India was home to his father's palace, where he was meant to begin each day's journey from the East. So Phaethon set out, full of joy and optimism. He told Helios about the humiliation he had to go through due to being accused of being an illegitimate child. He begged Helios to acknowledge him as his son and prove conclusively that he was the son of the Sun god. Deeply moved, Helios firmly confirmed Phaethon's legitimacy and paternity. He even said in front of everyone present that he would happily do his son any favors he requested.

Happy that the great Helios had acknowledged him as his son, Phaethon decided to put his father's love and generosity to the test. The brazen boy requested permission to drive the magnificent Chariot of the Sun for a single day. Concerned about his son's absurd request, Helios tried to persuade him that not even the powerful Zeus, much less a simple mortal, could pilot the Chariot of the Sun. Only the god Helios received that challenging assignment.

Unfortunately, they could not retract or change their minds once the gods committed. However, Helios tried in vain to convince the hurried Phaethon to back off from making his absurd demand. It was one thing to want to pilot the magnificent Chariot of the Sun, but to actually pull it off was more difficult than our naive Phaethon had anticipated.

As soon as he set off, Phaethon realized he had bitten off more than he could chew. The vicious horses began to follow a wild and dangerous course once they grasped the immaturity and inexperience of their young charioteer, and he discovered that he was entirely unable to control them.

The unstoppable Chariot of the Sun began to descend too low, and as it did, it crashed into the planet and unleashed a torrent of calamity, burning the African continent until it was a desert, causing terrible damage to the Nile River, and even turning the Ethiopians black from exposure to the Sun's fire.

Zeus was furious. All this destruction by the insolent boy made him fume. He struck Phaethon with a thunderbolt to prevent anything else, and the dead boy washed into the Eridanus River, subsequently known as the Italian River Po.

A Message for the Maldekian Starseed

Dear Maldekian Starseed, you are a wonderful person whose role in life is to help others. You may feel sad or angry at the world because of things that have happened to you, but don't let that overwhelm you. Your task is to help heal the planet and defeat evil forces wherever they appear. You have always known who you were and what you were meant to do, but now it's time for everyone else to know who you really are.

You'll be called crazy, and many people will attempt to silence your voice of truth, but you'll continue to speak your truth anyway. The people of Maldek are not who they seem to be, but neither are the world's ruling classes. You can see through their facades and deceptive masks when others can't. Your mission is to expose their true intentions and bring justice to those oppressed for far too long.

Your journey will not be easy, but it will be worth it. You'll encounter obstacles and challenges along the way, but you must stay strong and never give up. Remember that you are not alone in this fight; there are others who share your vision and will stand by your side. Together, you can create a better world for future generations. It's time to step into your power and fulfill your destiny as a warrior of light. The universe is waiting for you to make your mark and leave a lasting impact on this planet. So go forth with courage and determination, knowing you have the strength to accomplish anything you set your mind to. Believe in yourself and trust that your actions, no matter how small, can make a difference. The world is waiting for you.

Chapter 12: Avian Starseeds

Those who belong to the Avian race are a class of celestial beings from an entirely different universe, not even another planet or galaxy. These prehistoric life forms were master geneticists and creators who significantly impacted the multiverse's diversity by seeding the universe with various species. This is why they came into our universe billions of years ago.

These beings originate from a completely different universe and reside in higher dimensions and alternate realities, typically in the sixth to twelfth dimensions. However, most of them continue to exist as an exclusive group in the twelfth dimension. They are descended from tiny birds, and because they participated in the seeding of our universe, we can say that the birds on our planets are a gift from these enlightened ones.

Aside from having a greatly enhanced sense of consciousness, they can see the more abstract and expansive images of the entire multiverse and travel throughout the cosmos and consciousness through thought. They have a reputation for being able to communicate telepathically and mentally and have even created their own secret language. They carefully consider what worlds they will inhabit using this technique and then project themselves into the chosen world to establish themselves as resident lifeforms.

While their essence is incorporeal and spiritual, they can create physical bodies by projecting the cosmic energy that they normally use for communication through thought into the matter of a living planet. The world's religions, theologies, mythologies, and histories all prominently feature the Avians' involvement in life on Earth. We find them in the descriptions of the Tetramorphs and the Cherubim in a variety of sacred texts from various religions.

The frequent mentions of creatures with human, lion, ox, and eagle-like faces reveal this. One passage from the Holy Bible that illustrates this is Ezekiel 10:14, which states, "Each of the cherubim had four faces: One face was that of a cherub, the second the face of a human being, the third the face of a lion, and the fourth the face of an eagle. In terms of Starseeds, we can draw some further interesting parallels between the lion and the reincarnated Lyran, the human beings and the Anunnaki, and the eagles and the Avians. Not only that, but all the way up to the book of Revelation, they can be repeatedly found, as in Revelation 4:7, which states, "The first living creature was like a lion, the second was like an ox, the third had a face like a man, and the fourth was like a flying eagle."

The eagle is one of the most iconic beasts in the book, serving as a sign of strength, power, vision, and even devastation. "But those who wait on the LORD shall renew their strength; they shall soar up with wings like eagles; they shall run and not be weary, and they shall walk and not faint," says Isaiah 40:31. This type of analogy may be found throughout the writings of Leviticus, Exodus, Deuteronomy, Proverbs, Job, and many more.

Even more intriguing is that this is a prevalent theme in most faiths, theologies, and myths stretching back to ancient Egypt and other ancient civilizations. The reference to winged creatures in the Bible is nearly identical to those found in the Egyptian pantheon in that many of them were humanoid with the faces of various birds of prey. This is represented in the Egyptian Gods and goddesses such as Ra, Horus, Thoth, Isis, and others. The ancient Egyptians also mummified millions of birds in Thoth's honor from 650 B.C. to 250 B.C.

The veneration of these sacred creatures also has relevance in Greek mythology, as seen by Zeus carrying a lightning bolt in one hand and a mighty Eagle extending its wings in the other. It is also evident in Mesopotamian mythology with Marduk's association with the eagle, symbolizing his power and authority. The Eagle was worshiped as a divinity in ancient Islam, and they even worshiped an Eagle statue. There are numerous allusions to the griffin, which has many similarities in Persian myths and even in European, Anatolian, and many other cultures.

Avian Starseeds

According to estimates, there are only between 100 and 1000 of the Avian and Blue Avian Starseeds worldwide, making them the rarest group of Starseeds. They are a family of interdimensional heavenly entities that remain relatively mysterious to humans. Like other Starseeds, they have their own form of hierarchy, with the Blue Avian at the top.

Avian Starseeds are among the oldest sentient lifeforms in the cosmos, and they are unmatched in terms of creativity—perhaps only by the Starseeds from Lyra. As mentioned, they naturally function and live in the sixth through twelfth dimensions of the cosmos, a sharp contrast to civilizations like ours, which normally exist in the third to fifth dimensions. For this reason, they feel virtually stuck operating inside the boundaries of our 3-5D physical environment, which explains why there are so few of them on Earth. They've been here before and have come back with the same call for peace and to assist humanity in overcoming evil forces and the global ruling Cabal.

Avian Starseeds, some of the oldest souls in the multiverse, are innovative thinkers, which originates from their multidimensional view of cosmology. Their skills and talents are well known and documented across the universe, and they're also master astrologists.

The most essential things to the Avian Starseed are independence, sovereignty, and honor. They appreciate and honor all sentient lifeforms, regardless of shape, size, or color, and they demand the same in return. One of the worst things you can do to an Avian is to try to restrict them in any way. They are higher-dimensional beings that have transcended the dualism and physicality of our three-dimensional reality, and so they already feel uncomfortable in their bodies and third-dimensional environment. Denying them freedom and independence only increases their dread of being trapped.

Avian Starseeds, on average, have a sense of deep devotion to the Earth and the planet's people, but they also have a sense of right and wrong. They're well-versed in planetary affairs and care about the well-being of other sentient life forms and the global ecosystem. This is unlike humans, who are usually too self-centered to care about others.

Their skills and talents lie in the arts, religion, history, metaphysics, and the more spiritual aspects of our existence. Among their many contributions are their roles as guardians and protectors of sacred sites and artifacts and their service in maintaining the spiritual and astrological energy of the Earth. They are the ones who elevate vibrations at all levels of reality, from the individual to the cosmic. They are at the vanguard of expanding the boundaries of creativity and thinking and increasing the bar for developing greater levels of awareness, knowledge, and understanding.

Avians are here with a specific purpose: to bring about humanity's ascension to new levels of consciousness and awareness. They label their mission as the initiation of the Golden Age, which ultimately manifests as a global transformation of consciousness and humanity's transition into higher dimensions of universal evolution. They will bring into reality a new Earth by helping us rise above our current 3D existence into a new level of enlightenment through activating our dormant DNA codes, which hold all our potential for celestial divinity.

Characteristics of an Avian Starseed

- They are capable of seeing and understanding concepts that others cannot.
- They feel awkward being inside their bodies. They consider a 3D avatar extremely limited.
- They inspire humans to think bigger thoughts.
- They are acutely sensitive to colors, shapes, symbols, sounds, and vibrations.
- They have amazing memories and can recall any event or relationship with shocking clarity.
- They love the idea of bringing about a new Earth where they can experience freedom of thought and spiritual equality with all others from many different races, civilizations, religions, and creeds.
- They are masters at expanding consciousness through natural channels such as music, art, dance, conversations with others, different forms of meditation, and conscious breathing.
- They are obsessed with behavioral patterns. They can observe human behavior from many angles. A heightened state of awareness gives them the unique ability to observe these patterns closely and extrapolate them into predictions about how a person will respond in different situations.

- They are here to aid the free-spirited who feel like they have been misled due to the domination and suppression of the masses. They often seek out many different ways of life and many different religions, lifestyles, and ideologies. Freedom of expression is their top priority because they simply know that all living beings are equal and have the divine potential to explore new realms of thought and consciousness throughout the cosmos.
- They possess incredible creativity, both a gift and a curse in this realm. In addition to being creative thinkers themselves, they recognize that creativity is an important tool in uncovering solutions for humanity's problems at this time.
- They abhor violence as well as ignorance and those who practice it. They believe everyone should be treated with respect, kindness, and friendship.
- They seek help from mentors within this dimension. They are not interested in worldly power or wealth, which they perceive as an illusion, because they know that the truth lies in the realm of the Spirit.

A Message for the Avian Starseed

Dear Avian Starseed, you are here to assist in the transition into the New Earth. You are here to help humans move into a higher state of consciousness. You are about to experience levels of freedom beyond anything you have ever known before. Be grateful for your experience on Earth because it has helped you develop the flexibility and wisdom necessary for moving into a New Earth.

You have worked hard on this planet, and now it is time to rest your body and mind as you enter higher-frequency realms of existence. The New Earth is a place of pure love and light, where you'll be surrounded by beings of elevated consciousness who are here to support you on your journey. You'll no longer be bound by the limitations of the physical world but will instead be able to tap into the infinite potential of the universe. Every part of your body is imbued with divine intelligence, and you are able to create the life you want simply by imagining it. What you most desire from this lifetime is accessible to you now that the veil has been lifted from your eyes. You can see the higher realms that await you—a state of existence beyond human imagination.

Chapter 13: Lemurian and Atlantean Starseeds

Geologists and biologists invented the term "Lemuria" towards the end of the nineteenth century to explain why lemurs may be found not only on the island of Madagascar but also on the Indian subcontinent and the Malaysian islands. A prehistoric land bridge connecting these now-separated places would explain how the lemur population managed to move from one site to the other—a feat that appears inconceivable if large amounts of water are thought to have been crossed. As a result, the hypothetical land bridge was dubbed "Lemuria." Its existence was determined in a manner similar to how fringe scientist Ignatius Loyola Donnelly deduced the presence of Atlantis, with lemurs acting as civilizations.

The works of theosophist Helena P. Blavatsky and her followers include the most sophisticated description of Mu/Lemuria. The Book of Dyzan, an old book, contains the real account of Atlantis and Lemuria, according to Blavatsky. Tibetan masters—teachers and practitioners of the age-old human arts—revealed this book to her. The Hidden Doctrine, a classic of theosophy, was released in 1888 and contains Blavatsky's interpretations and extrapolations of The Book of Dyzan. This doctrine claims that life developed on Earth in a series of phases.

In every one of these phases, mankind manifested in different shapes and with varying traits. Each stage is called a *"Root Race,"* and the history of mankind follows the progression of our species through seven stages, giving rise to seven Root Races. We are currently in the fifth stage, with the sixth and seventh stages looming in the distance, and each race is linked to a distinct continent.

The "Imperishable Holy Land" is where man's history began, according to Blavatsky. This Holy Land has never experienced the destiny of other rising and falling continents. It is said that it will exist from the beginning of time until the end of time. There have been claims that the Imperishable Holy Land is allegedly located at the North Pole, claims that may have looked more plausible in the 1880s than they do now. Others have speculated that this remote country is truly inside the earth and may be accessed through a large hole at the pole.

The North Pole – believed by some to be the "Imperishable Holy Land."[14]

W. Scott-Elliot, a supporter of Blavatsky, said in The Lost Lemuria (1904) that the First Root Race of the Imperishable Sacred Land had corporeal bodies made of "astral substance" that, if we could see them at all, would have appeared to us as enormous phantoms.

Blavatsky refers to the second continent as "Hyperborea." As the Second Race arrived, Hyperborea—which at the time included the entirety of what is now known as Northern Asia—stretched out its lands southward and westward to meet them. Since the planet had not yet tipped over on its axis, this northern continent is believed to have never experienced winter. While slightly more substantial than their ancestors, Scott-Elliot claimed that Hyperboreans were still essentially shapeless. They had simple skeletal and organ systems and underwent asexual budding reproduction, but they would have been invisible to the human eye, just like the First Root Race. The last remnants of this race, which eventually disintegrated, are found in the Arctic Circle.

The Third Race, the Lemurian, developed from the etheric Second Race. Even though their vertebrate structure had not yet solidified into bones like ours, their bodies had become material and were made up of the gasses, liquids, and solids that make up the three lowest divisions of the physical plane. At first, they could not stand upright with bones as malleable as those of young infants today, but in time, they acquired a sturdy bony structure around the middle of the Lemurian epoch. With their newly acquired bodies, Lemurians became more human-like. They developed a language, and their history and culture began on the Indian subcontinent.

The Atlantis continent was the fourth one. A Root Race that appeared completely human lived in Atlantis. Although most historians disregard the ancient record of Atlantis' existence, Blavatsky suggests that it should be considered the first historical continent. In The Story of Atlantis, Scott-Elliot provides thorough descriptions of Atlantean life and culture. Humanity first displayed cultural development, including literacy, the arts, science, and religion.

According to Scott-Elliot, the education provided to the exceptionally talented children of Atlantis included instruction in using psychic abilities and the occult healing powers of plants, metals, and precious stones. They learned how to harness the magical powers of the universe as well as the alchemical processes of matter transmutation. He talks about the amazing technological advancements made by the Atlanteans, such as flying machines and airships. The wealthy class intended to use these airships.

From two-seaters to ships with room for eight, they were typically constructed for a small number of people. However, these ships were employed in combat as the Atlantean age descended into warfare. These battleships were significantly bigger and could carry up to 100 sailors. They could travel at an elevation of several hundred feet and reach speeds of 100 miles per hour.

Unlike the earlier Lemurian Root Race, the Atlantean civilization contained organized religion. They held the concept of a Supreme Being represented by the sun. On hilltops where rings of upright monoliths were constructed, this sun-deity was worshiped. These monoliths, the surviving example of Stonehenge, were also used for astronomical rituals. As the end of Atlantis approached, the continent underwent a period of cultural degradation. Peace and prosperity led to strife and violence, and the sun's worship devolved into fetishism. The continent eventually sank beneath the ocean, and the once-great Atlantis was lost beneath the waves forever.

Atlantean and Lemurian Starseeds

These two ancient civilizations, now lost beneath the Earth's oceans, are said by some researchers to have left behind genetic and etheric DNA that is still a part of our collective consciousness. Also called Gaia Starseeds, they are the forefathers of our current civilization and continue to influence its destiny.

According to theosophists such as Alice Bailey, some Lemurian and Atlantean souls were advanced beings who achieved high levels of consciousness and now assist humanity from the unseen realms. They were thought to have originally lived in Atlantis and Lemuria but transcended to higher dimensions when these civilizations sank beneath the sea. Some of these souls were said to have incarnated on Earth in the 20th century and are alleged to have helped establish the New Age Movement and spread spiritual teachings.

These enlightened souls are believed to possess immense wisdom and knowledge, guiding humanity toward spiritual evolution and enlightenment. Through their subtle influence, they inspire people to explore their inner selves, embrace holistic healing practices, and seek unity with the divine. Lemurian and Atlantean Starseeds are seen as guardians of ancient wisdom, preserving esoteric teachings passed down through genetic coding. Their presence in the unseen realms serves as a reminder of humanity's potential for growth and transformation. As we navigate the complexities of modern life, their guidance offers solace and inspiration, reminding us to connect with our higher selves and embrace the interconnectedness of all beings. The legacy of these advanced beings continues to shape the spiritual landscape of our world, encouraging us to embark on a journey of self-discovery and transcendence.

Characteristics of Lemurian and Atlantean Starseeds

- **You Feel at Peace in or Around Water:** You feel at home near water, as if it holds a deep and profound significance for your soul. Whether it's the gentle lapping of waves against the shore or the tranquil flow of a river, being near water brings you a sense of calm and rejuvenation. You may find yourself drawn to bodies of water, seeking solace and clarity in their depths. This connection to water is a characteristic shared by both Lemurian and Atlantean Starseeds, as these ancient civilizations were deeply intertwined with the element of water. It is believed that Lemurians were highly skilled in harnessing the healing powers of water, using it for purification and spiritual growth. Similarly, Atlanteans were known for their advanced knowledge of underwater technologies and their ability to communicate with marine life. As a Starseed with these lineage connections, your affinity for water reminds you of your ancient origins and your innate ability to tap into its wisdom and energy.

- **You are Skilled in the Healing Arts:** It is believed that those Starseeds who originated from Atlantis or Lemuria inherited certain healing methods from their lineage. These ancient civilizations were known for their advanced scientific knowledge, and it is hypothesized that these techniques could have been passed down through generations of Starseeds, allowing them to harness the earth's energy and healing properties. As an Atlantean or Lemurian Starseed, you'll likely be talented in the spiritual healing arts, drawing on your ancestry's heritage to maximize your natural abilities. Some of the ancient Atlantean and Lemurian healing practices that may have been passed down to you include methods for purifying water and harnessing its energy for spiritual growth, the art of crystal healing, vibrationally-oriented therapies like reiki, and etheric energy manipulation.

- **You Are Sensitive to Nature:** Those who descended from the ancient civilizations of Lemuria and Atlantis are often deeply attuned to the energy of nature, possessing a powerful connection with animals and plants. This sensitivity is likened to that of a psychic, allowing you to "feel" the presence of animals and plants around you. Your sensitivity is an innate talent that may have been cultivated in past lifetimes when Lemurians were known for their advanced psychic abilities and Atlanteans were renowned for their intuitive abilities. As a Starseed, your ability to connect with nature may cause you to develop into an accomplished healer and naturalist.

- **You Are Grounded:** You have a strong connection with the Earth and its chakras. Your essence is rooted and grounded in nature, so you are highly attuned to the planet's energy vibrations. You are often drawn to the natural world for inspiration and guidance, preferring to spend time outdoors in nature rather than indoors. Additionally, your personality may be highly influenced by Earth's energies, as some Starseeds born of these lineage connections are prone to experiencing life-changing revelations when spending time in nature.

- **You Have an Affinity for Crystals:** It is believed that in past lifetimes, Atlanteans and Lemurians were skilled in the art of crystal healing. This ancient healing practice emphasized the power of crystals to cleanse and revitalize human energy fields, restore health, and release negative energy. Lemurian Starseeds are often drawn to crystals for spiritual guidance and healing purposes and may be drawn to them as part of their metaphysical practice. The Lemurians' affinity with crystal healing dates back to their early Stone Age culture, when they used crystal power to cure illness, navigate the sea, and communicate with spirit guides.

A Message for the Lemurian and Atlantean Starseeds

Dear Lemurian and Atlantean Starseeds, you may experience a burning desire for spiritual evolution and expansion as you awaken to your divine purpose. You may feel drawn to explore your inner self through the healing arts, becoming a healer of substance and integrity. You are here to become an advocate for holistic healing practices, encouraging others to embrace the transformative power of nature for emotional and physical growth. As you continue down this path, be sure to incorporate both science and spirituality into your lifestyle, as these two principles have the potential for synergistic growth when balanced.

You may also find yourself drawn to water, with a deep connection likely passed down through genetic coding from Lemurian ancestors. Your ancestral lineage connections allow you to harness the element's energy for spiritual evolution and manifestation purposes. Water holds a profound healing energy that can be harnessed with the intentionality necessary to manifest your desires into reality. This deep connection gives you a wealth of inner guidance and wisdom, helping you cultivate your talents and manifest your dreams.

As you awaken to the truth within, you may remember a time when you mastered water-based arts in a culture that revered the power of the element. You may feel connected to this ancestral legacy, growing curious about your Lemurian or Atlantean origins. This is a sign that you are ready to tap into your soul purpose and expand your consciousness beyond the physical world's limitations. You are being called to become a force of healing and connection, bringing love and health to the world. When you embrace this calling, you'll spark a transformation of consciousness that can ripple through the planet, healing those around you and awakening them to their own divinity.

Chapter 14: Your Earthly Mission

This final chapter aims to guide Starseeds who are awakening to their planetary missions and challenges as they traverse the physical realms of Earthly life while remembering who they are. You need to remember, reconnect, and then discover the gifts you have been given to share with humanity. The world needs a shift in consciousness where we feel connected to each other again and can support each other with love, compassion, and patience. As a Starseed, you are here to assist in this shift. You may need to adjust your vibration at times, as the energies of this world can feel very heavy, dense, and difficult to handle. In fact, many Starseeds are on Earth for the first time and have no

For you to become a successful Starseed, you need to find your purpose.[13]

idea how to navigate their unique personalities and the challenges they face in their nascent earthly lives. As with any culture shock, there can be a sense of being overwhelmed and unsure of how to fit in. But here is the secret: You don't have to fit in. You can create and receive whatever you need to fulfill your mission. This is a beautiful thing. You can also choose not to accept any of the challenges you face. They can indeed feel substantial sometimes, but many times the lessons they teach you are what you need to reclaim your true self.

As a Starseed, you are a consciousness of light and love. You are here to be a beacon of guidance for humanity, and the most delightful thing is that you won't have to deal with people who are not ready for the love that you give freely, which is unconditional. You are here to bless the earth and to uplift and assist humanity with your love, wisdom, and light. You are here to create beauty in the world. You can heal, restore, and replace what is not serving the universe in any way.

Remember that you are not alone and that you are being supported by the collective consciousness of Starseeds who have gone before you. Whatever your Starseed mission entails, some of the things you may experience include:

- Feeling overwhelmed by new and unfamiliar experiences all at once.
- Experiencing energy shifts, both positive and negative, within your body.
- Having a sense of déjà vu, knowing that you have been here before.
- Feeling disconnected from humanity and alien to the world you live in.
- Realizing that your life is not what it seems, and your soul mission is challenging your current reality.
- Feeling judged by others for the choices you make or the way you express yourself.
- You may feel confused about your purpose on Earth because things here are very different from where you have come from. You are a unique person, making it challenging to understand the ins and outs of human behavior and what is accepted as "normal" here on Earth.

- You may feel like you are seen as weird or different, or people may criticize the things you do. It helps to remember that what is weird and different here on Earth is special and unique elsewhere in the Cosmos.

Many Starseeds are being tested for their self-worth and self-empowerment. Being a pioneer of any kind is tough in this world where we have been conditioned to accept limiting beliefs about our worthiness by those who believe they have the right to manipulate others to their will for the sake of power, control, and greed.

Sometimes you feel emotionally, mentally, and physically overwhelmed by the world around you. The key to maintaining your sanity is to support yourself in ways that align with your gifts and talents. Make sure you are not sacrificing what brings joy into your life just because others say it is not "realistic, practical, or useful" in reality. This can be very challenging, but for you, it is all about being the shining light that you are. In this way, you are honoring your soul and your mission.

Protecting Your Energy Throughout Your Earthly Journey

Sometimes you may find yourself agitated by the people around you. You may feel like your purpose on Earth is being thwarted, or you may feel invisible and unheard. Things can be confusing, and sometimes you may feel very alone. As a Starseed, you are far more sensitive than most humans on Earth, as your consciousness has expanded in other worlds. You may find that emotions are more intense for you, especially negative ones like anger, fear, resentment, and sadness. The good news is that all these feelings will pass if you allow them to; they are not permanent fixtures in your life, even when they seem to be.

You must find ways to protect your energy from being manipulated by others. In this way, you can find the clarity of mind that you need to make sense of things so that your inner wisdom can guide you in the choices you make for yourself. To that end, these tips might help:

- Your first line of defense is your own mind. You have the power to control the thoughts you have. Understand that whatever you focus on, you attract more of it into your life. If you are worried, fearful, or anxious about a situation or people in your life, this thought energy doesn't serve you and will attract more situations that support these negative emotions. So, stay positive and focused on what brings light and love into your life.

- The next way to protect your energy is through meditation. You are already an expert in this art form, whether or not you realize it, so use it to guide you on the path of self-discovery and healing. Leave your mind open as you breathe in and out through your nose. As you do this, let everything you experience come and go without judgment or attachment. This allows your soul to connect with the present moment while also allowing it to send out loving energy into the world around you.

- Spend time in nature. This is one of the most grounding things you can do for yourself, as your energy will be lifted in the presence of trees, plants, and animals. Sunshine and fresh air also do wonders for raising your vibration.

- Surround yourself with supportive people who bring joy into your life. We all have relationships that no longer serve us, but sometimes it's hard to let go of these people because we don't want to be alone. This is where you can use your intuition to discern if a person in your life is good for you or not. You know the answer when you feel good and happy in their company instead of feeling drained or confused.

- When going through difficult emotional situations, take care of yourself first; leave the drama for later. You may have to let go of certain people in your life to take this step.

- Connect with a healthy support system of friends who are also Starseeds. They will understand the unique challenges you face and will be an invaluable resource in helping you stay grounded and positive.

- Research the benefits of alternative healing methods for your body and soul. Many alternative methods can be very beneficial in helping you clear negative energy from your etheric field. This is one of the best ways to protect and replenish your energy.

Connecting with Other Starseeds

You may or may not have a difficult time making friends. If you do, it is likely because you are unique, and people are not always comfortable with those who are unlike them. You may find it easier to make friends with people similar to you regarding ideologies or interests. You should consider reading more about other Starseeds to connect with them and feel less alone as you navigate this strange and alien earthly journey. Here are some strategies that can help you find a connection with other Starseeds:

- Get in touch with other Starseeds on the internet. Many YouTubers, mediums, and authors have written about being a Starseed that you can follow and learn from.
- Join an alternative spirituality forum or class in your area. You can meet like-minded people and share ideas and experiences in these places.
- Attend a spiritual festival or retreat that celebrates the diversity of spiritual knowledge across astrology, mythology, magic, energy healing, meditation, divination, and many other areas of study.
- Share your experiences with loved ones who support you unconditionally without judgment or criticism, even if they don't understand what you're going through.
- Go to a psychic or medium who specializes in working with Starseeds and lightworkers. They can offer you guidance and support as you unpack your soul mission and the challenges you face in this dimension.
- Start writing about your experiences on the internet. If you're a writer, this is a great outlet for expression and helps keep your thoughts in check as you navigate this transition process. You never know; you may discover that others share your views and experiences and want to connect with you.

Being a Starseed is not always easy, but it is an honor to be incarnated at this time to help promote unity, consciousness, and positive change in the world. You know you're a Starseed when you feel like you don't belong and also have a deep longing for true connection with your soul group and fellow Starseeds who can help guide you on this journey of self-discovery. As a Starseed, your mission is to explore the depths of your soul to bring healing, peace, and unity consciousness to the world. This means having the courage to deal with your deepest fears and darkest emotions before you can rise into the light of truth, co-creating with people from all walks of life to make this world a better place. It's an exciting opportunity to be alive, so embrace your cosmic nature and take hold of your true power as a soul that has traveled many galaxies and dimensions. As you come into alignment with who you truly are, you'll discover that the experience of being a Starseed is one of empowerment and freedom—a path forward filled with endless possibility, adventure, and growth.

How to Identify Your Starseed Mission on Earth

The experiences that you go through during this lifetime are very specific to the mission that your soul group has agreed to come to Earth to work on. This will be the catalyst for your spiritual evolution. You may be leading a normal life when suddenly, an event or experience triggers the awakening of your Starseed memories. This can occur through karmic connections with people from other lifetimes who are now in your life, books you read, films you watch, or events you attend at spiritual gatherings, all of which hold the seed of awakening within them. You may not even be aware of the exact purpose of your life when you encounter this catalyst. However, the universe will continue to provide you with clues and opportunities to seek out the answers. Below are some signs that can indicate your Starseed mission on Earth:

1. Suppose you find yourself drawn to a subject or an area of study that you feel is too new or mysterious to understand. In that case, that's a sign that your soul has activated the intelligence of a new possible incarnation.
2. Suppose you feel unsatisfied with your current career path. In that case, no matter how much money you make or how beloved and famous you are, this is a sign that your mission demands that you move on from where you are.
3. Suppose you experience a sudden change in your relationships with people or acquaintances. In that case, this is a sign that you are being telepathically and energetically connected to someone from another lifetime in preparation for a karmic reunion.
4. If you begin to feel that a huge transformation is occurring within your life and you have no idea why, then this is a sign that you are being guided toward some type of karmic gift or hidden purpose in your life.
5. If an event or experience causes you to question your present reality, then this is a sign that the awareness of another lifetime has been activated within your consciousness.

6. Suppose you find that low-vibrational people are karmically connected to you. In that case, this is a sign that your mission is to awaken the Starseed in them through your own actions and words.
7. If you find yourself having vivid dreams or visions about somewhere unknown, yet feel an intense attraction toward the images in these dreams, then this is a sign that your soul memories are drawing on nature spirits from another lifetime to help with the activation of your soul's mission.
8. Suppose you feel that many people are moving away from your path or against your actions. In that case, this is also another sign that your mission requires you to raise the consciousness of other people.
9. If you find yourself being deliberately pushed into spiritual or personal development classes, books, or workshops by family, friends, or seemingly random people, even if you are very resistant to it, then this can be a sign that your mission requires that you take part in this event or activity.
10. Suppose people you meet for the first time tell you about spiritual books, experiences, or movies that resonate with your personal and spiritual growth. In that case, you are likely Starseeds who recognize each other. You could also have been brought together to support each other in a karmic situation.

Your mission is one of service and self-discovery on the path of awakening and empowerment. It is to embrace your cosmic nature and live with courage and passion, even in the face of ridicule or doubt from others. Your mission is to awaken humanity to their true stellar origins through your words and actions, teaching them about their multidimensional abilities while inspiring them to unlock the mystery of love within themselves. This is why fitting into earthly society, career paths, or relationships can also be difficult. However, the deep sense of longing you may feel as a Starseed is nothing more than a signal to awaken your mission. And it is important to remember that these feelings are not permanent or even real. These experiences are part of the catalyst that allows you to come to terms with the emotions that have been stored and suppressed within you, probably for lifetimes. The more you can open up and talk about your experiences, the quicker you'll be able to resolve them and move forward on your mission. Being a Starseed is a path of fearlessness, trust, and adventure. It is an opportunity to flow with the cosmos while awakening the Starseed within other people and yourself.

Conclusion

Starseeds are the masters of consciousness in our solar system. They have been working on this planet for a long time and are not even vaguely near finished. These loving beings are the keepers of light, and they work tirelessly to see that the light remains shining until every human being wakes up to the truth. One way they are connected to us is through the structures of mass consciousness that they have created on Earth, which we refer to as religions. They created these religious structures lifetimes ago to help raise the frequency of the planet and expand humanity's spiritual awareness.

Each religion offers a unique path toward enlightenment, catering to humanity's diverse needs and beliefs. From Christianity to Buddhism and Islam to Hinduism, these religions serve as guiding principles for millions seeking spiritual growth. Rituals, prayers, and teachings provide a framework for understanding the mysteries of existence and connecting with the divine. The celestial beings behind these religions understand that humans learn and evolve at different paces, so they have tailored each faith to suit various cultures and societies. This diversity allows for a rich tapestry of beliefs and practices that ultimately lead towards the same goal: awakening to our true nature as spiritual beings.

As we engage with these religious structures, we tap into the collective wisdom and energy of countless souls who have walked this path before us. We become part of a vast network of seekers united by our shared desire for truth and enlightenment. The universe continues to guide us through subtle whispers, synchronicities, and intuitive nudges, always inching us closer to the realization of our true selves. Through our beliefs and practices, we align ourselves with the divine and open ourselves up to the guidance and support of our galactic family. They assist us in our journey of self-discovery, gently guiding us toward a deeper understanding of our spiritual nature. With their help, we continue progressing towards awakening and enlightenment, constantly growing and evolving on our path.

Together with the collective wisdom of those who have come before us, we embark on a transformative journey toward the ultimate goal of union with the divine. This journey has its challenges as we confront our limitations and face the shadows within ourselves. However, with the guidance of the universe and the support of our spiritual community, we find the strength to overcome these obstacles and continue on our path of self-realization.

As humanity delves deeper into their spiritual practice, they will learn to cultivate qualities such as compassion, gratitude, and forgiveness. These virtues become the foundation of their interactions with others and shape their relationships with the world around them. They will recognize that every being is interconnected and that by extending love and kindness to all, they are contributing to the collective awakening of their species.

You can develop a heightened sense of awareness and a deep connection to the present moment through meditation and contemplation. You can learn to quiet the incessant chatter of your mind and tap into a profound stillness within. In this state of inner peace, you can easily access higher realms of consciousness and receive divine guidance.

The spiritual journey is not just about personal growth and enlightenment but also about spreading love and kindness to others. By recognizing the interconnectedness of all beings, we understand that our actions have ripple effects that can contribute to the rise or fall of humanity as a whole. Therefore, we must cultivate compassion and empathy, treating everyone with respect and understanding. As we navigate life, we encounter challenges and obstacles that test our strength and resilience. During these moments, we must remember to stay grounded in our spiritual practices, drawing upon the wisdom and guidance we have gained along the way.

By staying connected to our inner selves, we can find clarity amidst chaos and make decisions that align with our higher purpose. We continue to evolve and grow through self-reflection and introspection, shedding old patterns and beliefs that no longer serve us. This continuous process of transformation allows us to embody our true essence and live authentically. As we walk this spiritual path, we inspire others to embark on their own journey of self-discovery and awakening. Together, we create a collective consciousness rooted in love, compassion, and unity. Through this collective effort, we can bring about positive change and a new Earth.

Part 2: Pleiadian Spirituality

Secrets of the Pleiades, Astrology, and Messages from the Pleiadians

Introduction

The fact that you are reading this right now says one thing about you: You are a seeker of light. *It isn't a coincidence that you found this book.* You will embark on a journey that will change you in unexpected ways. You are about to dive deep into Pleiadian spirituality – and not one person who has dipped a toe in this vast ocean has come out of it the same way. But don't worry, because you can rest assured that the transformation you experience will be so amazing that you wonder how you could possibly have lived your life for so long any other way.

The pages of this book invite you to come along on a stellar journey that goes beyond the boundaries of what is already known. This book is an invitation to the vast realms of the Pleiades. To some, the Pleiades are nothing more than a star system, at best, to be admired and, at worst, ignored. However, there is much more to that system than meets the eye. This system has fascinated mystics, seekers, and dreamers since ancient times. Pleiadian stars have many secrets to share, and their ancient wisdom is unparalleled.

This book is unlike any other on the topic of Pleiadian spirituality out there. Written in simple-to-understand English, the messages within are easy to grasp. You will also find this book packed with techniques and tools to help you connect with your Pleiadian ancestry. The methods for exploring your Pleiadian spirituality are easy. That means you won't be left scratching your head in confusion about what to do.

The secrets of the Pleiadians are available to those with open hearts and receptive spirits. You will discover the profound teachings and insights that the majestic Pleiadian beings have to share with humanity. These teachings will lead to the ultimate evolution of the Earth into what it was supposed to be: a glorious, beautiful world, a welcoming home for all beings in the cosmos.

Deep within your soul, you resonate with the Pleiadian energies. While you may not know it right now, something in you is strongly connected to the cosmic group of beings that call the Pleiadian star cluster home. You will learn that you are literally made of star stuff, which means you are divinity in the flesh. It is time for you to awaken to who you really are. It is time for you to become aware of the spiritual potential you carry.

As you read this book, you will be equipped with the tools to discover yourself and to remember all the pieces of your soul. Think of the pages as a portal that connects you directly to your Pleiadian ancestry and the teachings of these timeless beings. If you are ready to radically transform your life and step into your role as a Pleiadian Starseed, what are you waiting for? *Dive right in.*

Chapter 1: Welcome to the Pleiades

For a moment, assume you have the power of flight. It's time to go on a journey that will change your life. You're standing outside when you lightly tap your foot against the ground, and that little movement lifts you into the air, where you remain suspended. You propel yourself toward the big blue sky with white fluffy clouds reminiscent of cotton candy. You continue to soar, cutting through the clouds, shivering a little at the feeling on your skin as you move. But it's a good feeling. You continue, moving upward, gaining momentum, feeling the wind whip against your face. The air is thinner here, but it's all good. Somehow, you can still breathe. Somehow, you feel more alive than ever before.

Now, you're in space. You continue your journey, looking in awe at the heavenly bodies in the universe. You're traveling at the speed of light when, bam! You come to a sudden stop. All around you are brilliant stars in the hundreds, shining brightly and beautifully. You're now 444 light-years away from Earth, hovering in the middle of the Pleiades, a constellation that is part of a larger star cluster known as the Taurus constellation. There you are, in the flesh, with the Seven Sisters.

Astronomical Facts about the Pleiades

The Pleiades.[16]

Also known as M45, the Pleiades can be seen from Earth from the middle of June to early May. You may not be able to fly, but if you're ever in the Northern Hemisphere, you can see the stars at night from October and throughout winter. This star system is 444.2 light-years away. A light-year is the distance light travels in a year, which is 5.8 trillion miles.

Sure, the stars are called the Seven Sisters, but there are over 1,000 stars in the cluster. Some stars shine bright enough that light reflects on the blue dust and gas nebulae around. Six stars are so bright you can see them without a telescope. Galileo Galilei was the first to closely examine the Pleiades using a telescope. He spotted over 40 stars in that cluster. The first photograph was taken in 1885 by Paul and Prosper Henry.

The Mythology of Pleiades

Thanks to the high visibility of this star cluster, the Pleiades is significant to many cultures. The Vikings saw the stars as Freyja's hens. Greek mythology says they were the seven daughters of Atlas, the Titan. Since Atlas was saddled with the punishment of holding the sky in place for all eternity, he couldn't keep his daughters safe from Orion, the hunter, who sought to rape them. Zeus tried to help by turning Atlas's daughters into stars. Sadly, this did nothing to stop Orion, who also became a constellation. Now he chases the Seven Sisters through the sky. What are the sisters' names? Alcyone, Maia, Electra, Merope, Taygete, Celaeno, and Asterope or Sterope. Their mother is Pleione, the sea goddess. Some of the gods of Olympus would be engaged to the sisters. The youngest sister was Merope, and she would later marry Sisyphus. Her marriage made her mortal, and she faded away, and this is why one star doesn't shine as brightly as the other six.

The Europeans of the Bronze Age believed the cluster had to do with funerals and mourning as it would rise in the east while the sun set during Samhain or Halloween – when the dead would be remembered and celebrated. The Mexican and Central American Aztecs' calendar was connected to the Pleiades. They saw the star cluster as a sign that the new year was at hand, and they always kicked off the new year when the Pleiades came up right before the sun. This phenomenon was known as the *heliacal rising*, which mattered to many ancient cultures, as it was the start of the planting season. This is also why Pleiades is associated with abundance and fertility.

The New Zealand Māori also held the Pleiades in high regard, as its rising was the start of the new year. They called the star cluster *Matariki*, and it was the herald of feasts and celebration, as well as a time to honor the dead. Matariki is a mother, with the other six stars as her daughters.

In Aboriginal mythology, the Seven Sisters are called the *Napaltjarri sisters*. The desert was their home, and they lived with their father, who was a legendary hunter. Things changed when Jilbi Tjakamarra came to the desert and was smitten by the sisters. He had magical powers, which he used to make the sisters fall for him, but they weren't interested.

Eventually, they had to run and hide from Jilbi. The sisters journeyed to Uluru, where they took a break to look for honey ants. No sooner had they arrived than Jilbi caught up with them. They were tired of running, scared of the man who wanted them by any means necessary, and at a loss for what to do about their predicament. So, they turned to the Uluru spirits, who offered to help them. The Uluru spirits turned the sisters into stars and placed them in the night sky. This made Jilbi very upset. He would eventually turn himself into the Morning Star, which is on Orion's belt, so he could continue chasing the sisters – as he still does today.

The North American Sioux also have their own legend about the Pleiades. They say it is connected to the Devil's Tower. They hold that the stars were seven women running away from a bear. They reached out to the gods, who answered their prayers by raising the ground beneath their feet into the air so the bear couldn't reach them. Then, these women became stars.

To Hindus, the Big Dipper constellation of stars was known as the *Rishis*. The Rishis were wedded to seven sisters called *Krittika*. At first, they were all happy together in the northern sky. But then, Agni, the fire god, fell in love with the Krittika. He did his best not to act on it and even took off into the forest to avoid them. In the forest, he found Svaha, the Zeta Tauri star. Svaha was smitten by him and wanted his love by any means possible. So, she wore a disguise to look like six of the Krittika, and Agni was hooked. Svaha would give birth to a child, and with time, it was rumored that the six Krittika were his mothers. When this rumor got to the Rishis, they divorced their wives. The only wife who remained married to her husband was Arundhati. Her husband is the star called Alcor. As for the other six ex-wives, they would go on to become the Pleiades.

Who Channels the Pleiadians?

The Pleiadians are extraterrestrials who speak through channels as a stream of collective consciousness. Barbara J. Marciniak first channeled them. She had always been interested in metaphysics, which she studied intensely. In her work, she credits The Seth Material, a book written by the entity known as Seth, channeled by the late Jane Roberts. Thanks to The Seth Material, Barbara learned all she needed to make a conscious connection to the Pleiadians. This avid traveler would first channel the Pleiadians in May 1988 in Athens, Greece, after she'd had a deep, spiritual experience at the Great Pyramid of Giza. Now that you know about channels, what about the aliens themselves?

Who Are the Pleiadians?

The Pleiadians are humanity's ancestors because they were here long before humans existed. Some of the Pleiadians wanted to be part of the creation and maintenance of Earth, so they incarnated on Earth as humans, too. Many wanted to participate in the experiment meant to turn the Earth into an intergalactic center full of peace and light. Unfortunately, things haven't gone according to plan, and humanity is suffering for it. Pleiadians have made contact with humanity to help the Earth and its people heal from this suffering. Those in contact with Pleiadians learn how to shift from the three-dimensional world (Earth) to higher-dimensional worlds that cannot yet be perceived with the current scientific tools.

The reason Pleiadians are assisting humans in learning to make this shift to higher realms is that doing so will assist with the ascension of the race so that it can be what it was originally meant to be: a loving, peaceful people aware of and in touch with the multidimensional aspects of their Soul. This would mean finally, humans could create a world free from the chaos and tyranny that plagues the present Earth.

During the formation of the Earth, which they refer to as *Terra*, some of them wanted to incarnate here so they could experience what it would be like to recreate as humans. Their society is rooted in love, which is something humanity sorely needs. These aliens have the same technology we do. They work with computers. However, that's where the similarity in our technology ends, as they are many miles ahead of us with their abilities.

The Pleiadians have the technology to transport themselves from 444.2 light-years away to Earth quicker than you can imagine. They also have various means of transportation but will mostly make this trip to Earth using starships they call "mother ships." These vessels stretch about a mile long, serving as home to thousands of Pleiadians. They can make it to Earth from the Pleiades in days. They also have disc ships that travel faster than the mother ships, making the trip in hours.

It's not easy for the Pleiadians to work with the human system of timing things because hours and minutes aren't experienced the same for them. Pleiadian technology is far more advanced than that which is available to humans. It is ancient, with origins from a different universe that has evolved to the point of returning to the source of all things, which the aliens call "*First Cause.*" The only reason Pleiadians have chosen to forgo this evolution is because they are deeply invested in the growth of humanity. So, they were permitted to share what they know because all their technology is rooted in principles that agree with the First Cause, and they aren't given to acting in ways that don't line up with love and growth.

Humans aren't the only ones in contact with Pleiadians. They work with other solar systems that have their own unique beings. The Pleiadians say the whole universe is an experiment where every being has free will but that humans don't have a fundamental grasp of what free will is really about. They say it's about the idea that whatever you desire, you may have. You can do whatever you want. That is the point of existing in this universe.

Terra's Goal, According to the Pleiadians

Terra, or Earth, was created for specific reasons. It was meant to be a trade center for the solar system. Think of Earth as being like the various ports in different cities. It was meant to set the trends and be the hotbed of cultural and ideological progress. However, Terra would eventually deviate from this.

The Earth was meant to be the universe's crown jewel, the epitome of beauty. It was meant to allow the exchange of ideas, the growth of love and freedom, and a home to all creatures in the universe. Unfortunately, that is not the case. Unprecedented events happened that derailed the original plan. Things changed because the principle of free will cannot be violated, meaning that there can't be firm expectations about how things will go. However, the Pleiadians assure everyone that there's no reason to mourn that because change is coming.

In the very distant past, millions of years ago, a force would come along to disrupt the original goal of Terra's creation. This force was just another experiment, playing out another form of existence. You may be tempted to think of it as an evil force, but from the Pleiadian perspective, it's just another way of being and seeing things. This alien race is particular about maintaining a neutral stance regarding all subjects.

The force had a tremendous effect on Earth and created confusion in all universal hierarchies. Many attempts have been made to correct its course ever since this force came to be. The Pleiadians have been working with other higher spirits from First Cause. They offer their services freely with love because they have family trapped here, a family with whom they lost contact since the disruptive energies interfered with Earth's intended course.

The Pleiadian Goal

Losing touch with family would deeply trouble anyone, as you can imagine. The Pleiadians never considered that this could happen and have been deeply saddened and troubled by this loss. These highly evolved beings deeply rooted in First Cause know that the loss is only temporary and not a death sentence. However, it has been millions of years since this occurred. So terrible was the shock that it rocked multiple universes. However, they've got a plan to get back together with their family, and part of that plan is raising human awareness about life beyond Earth.

The Pleiadians have one chief goal: Retrieval. The target? Humanity. To achieve this, they have reconnected with people who are open and willing to work with them. This way, they can help everyone else find their way back to their true selves, free themselves from the current oppressive system, and either choose to remain on Terra or return to the Pleiades. When everyone is aware of the truth of their existence and the origins of Earth, raising the vibrational energy of the planet will become easy and allow Terra to evolve into what it was meant to be.

With the current state of the Earth, it might be difficult to imagine that it was meant to be so much more than it is. Take a good look around. You may find it incredulous to think that the objectives for Terra could ever be accomplished. However, the Pleiadians assure humanity that certain things are happening to correct its course. Long before now, these aliens knew that humans would eventually be ready to be contacted. The hope was that when the time came, humanity would be open to energy adjustments. Humanity's energy needs to be realigned to its true purpose. It was never part of the plan to force this realignment on people. Remember, the concept of free will is one that the Pleiadians deeply respect.

However, these trying times have worsened over the past four decades. The state of affairs on Earth is even more concerning to other beings in the universe. It has not done a great job of demonstrating love toward one another, and on top of that, humans have failed to view themselves as one. Humanity has allowed itself to fall prey to divisiveness on an individual and a collective level. Realize that what affects one affects everyone, and the Pleiadians are working hard to help humans wake up to this truth. Fortunately, the number of people waking up to who they are continues to grow. They are becoming aware of the First Creator, the source of who they are. They realize that the Creator sees no such thing as division or preference.

The fact that you are reading this now implies that you are one of those who are awakening. It will be your job to help others wake up to the truth. As dark as things may seem, the light continues to shine brighter and brighter. Eventually, humanity will know this light and love energy. If you feel a lot of confusion right now, this is fine. Usually, those who must wake up feel lost in their waking life, but they do lightwork in their dreams. When you are fully awakened, you will realize there is a great power within you. You will feel a strong sense of direction.

Waking up means you will need someone to show you the ropes. Think of it like being Neo in The Matrix, having Morpheus by your side to show you the truth. As you read this book, you are starting to peel back the layers of lies to reveal the truth. When the truth blooms within you, you will find yourself drawn to waking up others around you. If this sounds daunting, you don't have to be afraid. You will not experience this process alone because you have spirit guides, ascended masters, star families, and other universal forces working with you to achieve the same goal. However, you must be willing to play your part because your free will not be violated. You must also understand that respecting others and their wishes is paramount. You cannot force others to wake up before they're ready, so do not be frustrated if you are not getting immediate results.

In the next chapter, you'll learn more about Starseeds. What are the characteristics of Pleiadian Starseeds? What are their traits? What drives them? To learn more about this, continue to the next chapter.

Chapter 2: Pleiadian Starseeds

Most elements in human life come from the stars.[17]

Who Are Starseeds?

Dr. Timothy Leary was the first ever to use the word "Starseed" when referring to the drawing of the remains of an extraterrestrial discovered on a meteorite that hit the Earth. He wasn't talking about Starseeds in the same context as this book is. A Starseed has lived in some other place and time than here on Earth. Starseeds know there's something much grander than them in which they are meant to play a part. They know that everything and everyone is connected, so they don't assume that they or anyone else is at the heart of life. They know that life is much grander than anyone could comprehend.

Starseeds are aware that they exist in multiple dimensions, so they don't fall into the trap of assuming all there is to them is the life they lead on this little blue dot. If you are a Starseed, you know you're not your body, mind, or ego. You're not the stories you've come to believe about yourself or what you do at work. There are multidimensional layers to you — and everyone else — but you are more aware of that than the others around you. Sometimes, Starseeds are born with this awareness of the fullness of their being. Other times, they have to be awakened.

Ask an awakened Starseed, and they'll tell you they know their current incarnation is only one piece of the puzzle, just a few seconds of the infinity that is their soul's existence. These people are all over the Earth, on a grand mission to help everyone else awaken to who they are. Usually, they're the loners or those who know deep inside them that they'll never fit in no matter what they do or how well they wear their camouflage. The Starseed is the "weirdo" of the family or friend group. Some of these beings have been deliberately seeded into lands and families that do not see things the way they do. Without exception, they all have their assignments. If you're a Starseed, it may be your job to destroy old ways of doing things and upset the status quo. Or you may be here to bring in the new, wake others up, or prepare the path for the souls to come.

Without exception, Starseeds experience an event (sometimes traumatic) in their lives that leads to them waking up. This event happens at a young age and shows them how different they are from everyone else. Some respond to this awakening by doing their best to fit in, to wall off the bits of them that they think society would not accept. If you've awakened to the fact that there's something different about you, burying your uniqueness isn't a great strategy. Embrace what makes you different. Be courageous about being who you are because this is the only way to feel like you're living your true purpose.

Rooted in the Stars

Every human is made of star stuff. And no, that's not just some feel-good statement meant to motivate you to climb the corporate ladder to become the next Bezos or discover your inner Beyonce. According to Dr. Ashley King of the Department of Earth Sciences of the Natural History Museum, London, most elements in your body and life come from a star.

These elements took the stars billions of years to create. This may be why humanity has always looked to the stars for answers and with great wonder.

Humanity has always looked to the stars for answers.[18]

Around the world, some legends and myths talk about how life came to be and how everyone is connected to the stars. The Egyptians of old found that the flooding of the Nile happened simultaneously with the rise of Sirius each year (Sirius being the brightest star in the sky). Look through old Egyptian texts, and you'll find that the gods were from the stars. Isis descended from Sirius, Osiris from Orion, and so on. Study the alignment of the Pyramids of Giza, and notice how they line up with Mintaka, Alnitak, and Alnilam, the three stars on Orion's belt.

How about Mesopotamia? If you look at the Sun, Moon, and Quetzalcoatl pyramids in Teotihuacan, you'll find that they are perfectly lined up with Orion's Belt, too. The legends claim that the gods came down to Terra at this spot. Consider the Neolithic Avebury henge of the United Kingdom's Wiltshire. Look up the stone circle, and you'll find how it aligns with the Milky Way and how Stonehenge is set up so that the sun's first rays can hit it during the solstices.

If you're still not convinced that ancient man must have known something about humanity's connection to the stars, think about the fact that all over the world, there are so many places of worship set up to show some connection to the stars. For the past 40,000 years, Australian indigenous people have had their Dreaming stories about the stars, naming each and fitting them into their daily life. They would even use the celestial emu constellation to deduce the best time to look for emu eggs. The Mayans had stone temples in the Yucatan Peninsula that allowed them to observe the night sky above, and no one had a more precise astronomical calendar than they did.

Head over to West Africa, and look at the Dogon. You'll find that they celebrate the *Sigui* when Sirius collides with a landmark in the night sky. The tribespeople will also tell you that thousands of years ago, some beings came to visit them from Sirius. The Celts also have stories of how fairies came down to Earth from the stars. The Anasazi of Native America had settlements on three hills lined up with Orion in the sky. The Pawnee, Cherokee, Seneca, and Onondaga also have stories about the "Star Woman."

Across all these cultures, some vast distances apart, a starry thread connects humanity. Some people remember better than others that they didn't begin the adventure of life on Earth. These people know they come from other times and worlds. Some are Pleiadian Starseeds. There are other Starseeds, too. Let's take a quick look at some of them:

Sirians come from the planets around Sirius A (the brighter one) and Sirius B. Sirius A beings are actually from Vega, which is in the Lyra constellation. Sirius B is the home of the Merpeople and the Miengu, among others.

Arcturians are from Arcturus. These advanced beings are fifth-dimensional, like Pleiadians. They're excellent healers and shamans, and their realm feels angelic.

Andromedans are telepathic and dwell in the Andromeda Galaxy, also called M31. Their goal is to help the races enslaved by Reptilians. Science is their forte, and they're just as in touch with their emotions as they are with cold hard facts.

Indigo, Crystal, and Rainbow people have supernatural powers like clairvoyance, telepathy, clairaudience, reality shifting, etc. Indigo Starseeds have serious trouble witnessing injustice and letting it win. Crystal Starseeds feel the same but are kinder than the Indigo and Rainbow Starseeds. Finally, the Rainbow beings usually have autism in some form. All three Starseeds are not deeply connected to the physical world as it is but are in touch with their spiritual sides.

The Lightworkers come from various universes. They decided to reincarnate here to help humanity with the next phase of evolution. They're here to show love, light, and goodness to one and all.

Orion beings come from the eponymous constellation, and they're the ones who are curious and detail-oriented. They are very mental, love science and research, and want to help the Earth using their discoveries. They're not that great when it comes to matters of the heart. Some are here for good, while others seek to control the Earth, not set it free.

The Lemurians and Atlanteans are from Lemuria and Atlantis, ancient, advanced civilizations. Their spiritual technology would baffle the best and most brilliant scientific minds today. Unfortunately, these civilizations would eventually be destroyed by their complacency and greed. Some souls from these lands have returned to Earth to help avoid that same fate.

The Reptilians are also known as Draconians, Saurians, or Lizard People. With their shape-shifting abilities, they want to control and enslave the human spirit. According to David Icke, they continue to do so by working their way into politics and positions of power across various industries to manipulate society and direct the development of human culture.

Note that just because you're not a Pleiadian Starseed doesn't mean you don't have a role to play in the evolution of humanity. Everyone must play a part. Even the Reptilians, whether or not they're aware, will serve the goal of First Cause one way or another. After all, how would you know what's good if evil didn't exist?

Pleiadian Characteristics

If you're a Pleiadian Starseed, you've got Pleiadian DNA that will become active upon your awakening, and this will give you the keys to secret, ancient knowledge, and abilities you can use to help fellow Starseeds like you. You're likely in touch with your intuition. You love to learn and have no trouble picking up skills as if you have always done them. You're full of love and joy, more sensitive than most, and your creativity is off the charts. Little wonder, since you come from the star system known for teaching all other souls. Now, take a closer look at the characteristics of the Pleiadian.

Your energy is motherly. It doesn't matter if you're male or female. You have a soothing presence that is hard to ignore. It bothers you when someone isn't doing well, and your first instinct is to take the person under your wing and care for them. This is how you are towards people and nature in general.

You have unmistakable charm. People like you. Your charisma comes through effortlessly, and that's because you're at peace with your emotions and in tune with how others feel. You have no trouble connecting with others. Does this mean you're always the center of attention wherever you go? Not necessarily. However, your empathy will naturally draw people to you.

You have empathy. Boatloads of it. Whether you've gone through an experience or not, you can feel it in your body and soul. This is why people tell you everything, the truth, and nothing but. However, you may find yourself feeling constantly drained after interactions. You've got to know how to identify other people's feelings without taking ownership of them. Set clear boundaries while being kind. This way, you can recharge and continue to be of service to others.

You're sensitive. Being as empathetic as you are, this comes with the territory. It's a double-edged sword, your sensitivity. It's great because you can use it to help others feel understood, but it's not so great when you take other people's actions and words personally or see them more negatively than they are. Talk yourself through things before you react rashly.

You're open and giving. This brings you many friends — or people who want to think they're your friends. You help with no reservations and no expectations. The sad thing about this is the world has people who can recognize this trait in you and seek to drain you of everything they can. So you've got to learn discernment. Don't be quick to offer help to those you haven't taken the time to know, and also, if you get the hunch that someone is only using you, trust it. You tend to be a trusting person. Shady characters know it. To save yourself, you must trust yourself as much as you're willing to trust others. If your gut says to run from someone, run.

You can't help being honest. And this is something that many can't stand about you. You're at peace with realizing you were wrong about something and saying so right away. You don't mind letting people know that you don't know. You also are at home telling people like it is, without sugarcoating it. Those who listen will realize you're not being mean. In fact, your drive to always speak the truth comes from a place of love because you know you can't show up for others if you're not honest with them and yourself. But not everyone sees it that way.

You have people-pleasing tendencies. "Tendencies" may be putting it lightly. As a Pleiadian Starseed, you want everyone to get along, and you're not a fan of conflict and confrontation. This makes you susceptible to people-pleasing habits. You set yourself on fire to keep others warm, but that's not good because you'll burn out. That burnout will look like resentment and a desire to stay isolated behind a wall of ice. Know that you can still live harmoniously with people while being fair to yourself. Set boundaries, and realize that your self deserves the love and care you give to others, too.

You get competitive and seek perfection. These traits have their pros and cons. You find yourself striving to be the best at whatever you do, and this keeps you pushing to find better ways to accomplish things. But, if you're not careful, you'll wind up sucked into a vortex of comparison and dissatisfaction. It's okay to have high standards. But understand that perfection is a never-ending journey. Since it never ends, it's okay to pause now and then. Stop and smell the roses.

You start off with a torrent and taper off to a drizzle. You want to succeed, but sometimes keeping the momentum is really tough. No matter what you're working on, you may eventually get distracted by the next shiny thing or grind to a stop because you can't find the motivation to keep going. You also throw in the towel when you feel overwhelmed. The fix is to take breaks and try to do only one thing at a time.

You're a spiritual person. You may not subscribe to any religion, but you know there is something powerful at work in all of life. You know there's more to life than you can detect with your physical senses. This is great because you can lean on this power when times are dark, knowing it will always be there for you. You also desire spiritual development, so the odds are you have some practice that helps you daily, whether it's prayer, meditation, or a nightly walk in the park.

You decide with your heart. Your head may come along for the ride, but in the end, your heart is judge, jury, and executioner. Sometimes this works out in your favor. However, you should beware of making the big decisions too quickly since you may find yourself in situations you'd rather not have to deal with.

You live your life with purpose. To live any other way would be disorienting for you. You'd quickly feel life is pointless. You may not even know your life's purpose. But the awareness that you'll figure it out soon keeps you going despite having doubts.

You refuse to witness cruelty and do nothing about it. This is wonderful, but your drive has a sad origin. You may have experienced something traumatic when you were younger that made you more compassionate. This means that even in the face of being ostracized or losing your life, you will speak up for the oppressed and do what you can to stop maltreatment. Your moral compass is unbreakable.

You might be anxious, depressed, or not proud of yourself. You're not alone. This happens to most Pleiadians, especially before they wake up or if they aren't acting in alignment with their soul. If you feel this way, you should seek professional help, as that's the only way to be equipped for the task ahead.

Quiz: Are You a Pleiadian Starseed?

Pick the option that feels like a match.

1. Are you sensitive to other people's emotions, absorbing them like a sponge?

    a. Yes, and it's overwhelming!

    b. Sometimes. But I can tell my feelings apart from others and manage them.

    c. No, I'm not in touch with or affected by how others feel.

2. Do you feel like you've got a task to accomplish on Earth related to healing?

    a. Absolutely! I believe I'm here for a powerful purpose: To help others heal.

    b. I'd like to help. But I wouldn't say it feels like a mission.

    c. No, I don't feel called to do anything special like that.

3. Do you sometimes look at the stars and feel a longing to "go back home?"

    a. Yes, I feel a strong tug in my heart to return to something I can't remember.

    b. Sometimes, but not often.

    c. No, Earth feels like home.

4. Do you make more heart-based decisions than head-based ones?

    a. Yes. I trust my intuition and always follow it without question.

    b. Sometimes. But I try to balance my gut feelings with logic.

    c. No, I lean on logic and facts alone to make decisions.

5. Would you consider yourself a healer?

   a. Yes, I have natural healing abilities and want to help others.

   b. I'm interested in healing but haven't really plunged into it.

   c. No, I don't think of myself as a healer.

6. Do you feel a powerful urge to put others before yourself?

   a. Yes, I always handle others' needs before mine.

   b. Sometimes. But I do my best to take care of myself, too.

   c. No, I take care of myself first, and then I can take care of others after.

7. Have you had a terrible, traumatic childhood experience that triggered your awakening?

   a. Yes, I experienced some trauma that helped me grow spiritually.

   b. I've had some challenges, but I wouldn't call them traumatic.

   c. No, I had a stable and uneventful childhood.

8. Do you strongly desire peace, justice, and love in the world?

   a. Of course! It makes my heart ache to see what humanity does to itself.

   b. I'd love a better world, but I don't let reality consume me.

   c. I'm not really concerned about global matters.

9. Do you have a profound connection to nature?

   a. Yes! I feel so much love for it. When I spend time in natural spaces, I feel whole.

   b. I appreciate the natural world. But I don't feel deeply about it.

   c. No, I don't care much about that.

10. Would you say you're likable, charming, and seen as highly intuitive?

    a. Yes, people think I'm charismatic and that I have strong intuition.

    b. People like me. But I don't think anyone would call me intuitive.

    c. No, I don't have charisma or intuition.

Results

Mostly As: You are a Pleiadian Starseed! You have values that align with the Pleiadian way of life.

Mostly Bs: You have some Pleiadian traits, but the connection isn't strong. You may be a blend of Pleiadian and other Starseed energies (yes, this is possible). You'll need more research to figure out where you stand.

Mostly Cs: You're likely not a Pleiadian Starseed. You may be a different Starseed, or even a contactee, though.

Now you know who you are, what does it mean to see life through the eyes of a Pleiadian? How can you learn what their messages are? What themes do Pleiadians explore, and why does the wisdom Pleiadians share with one and all matter? You'll have these burning questions answered in the next chapter.

Chapter 3: Pleiadian Wisdom

The Pleiadians have continued to share much wisdom about how you can experience spiritual growth and develop yourself as a human. Diving into their teachings is the right choice because it means you can play your part in the evolution of the collective.

Pleiadian beings are particular about teaching inner transformation, unity, and love through channeling. The channel is a human being who will typically sit in silence and allow their vibration to come to a frequency that matches that of the entity to be channeled. Barbara Marciniak was the first to channel information from the Pleiadians and has written several books, including *Bringers of the Dawn: Teachings from the Pleiadians*, published first in 1992. Her book is packed with information from the Pleiadians about their purpose and the insights they've gained so far about humanity. Barbara is not the only one who channels the Pleiadians. In fact, if you have pure intentions and are willing, you, too, can serve as a channel.

The Pleiadian Teachings

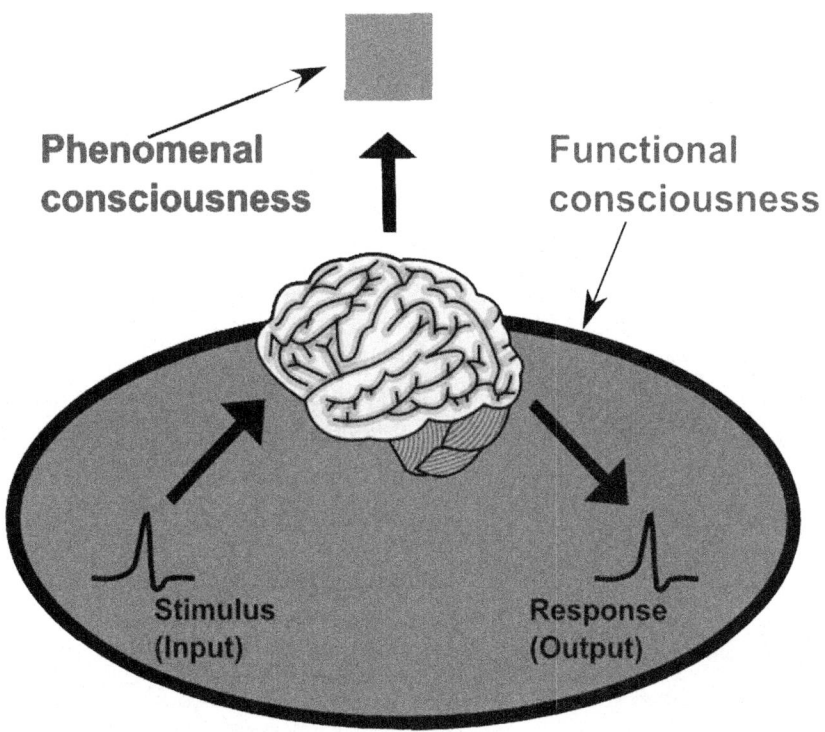

The law of consciousness is one of the most prominent Pleiadian teachings.[19]

The Pleiadians believe you should know the universal laws and do your best to use them. The laws are collectively called the 12 divine laws of the Pleiadians. Once you master the universe's laws, you will have mastered yourself and the world. The laws the Pleiadians espouse align with quantum physics, except that they know much more than Earthly scientists have yet discovered.

Think of the universe as a computer. Every part of it does the same thing as the parts of a computer but on a grander scale. This computer, like artificial intelligence, is sentient. It has all the information required to ensure the smooth operation of life. The universal laws are like the code that keeps the computer running as it should. If you do not know or follow the laws, you will not get the results in your life's endeavors. Without further ado, here are the 12 Divine Pleiadian laws.

Law 1: Consciousness is the source of all things and the cause of all things. This is the first cause from which every other thing arises. At the core of everything is consciousness, and there is nothing else. This consciousness is also known as energy and can neither be created nor destroyed. The only thing you can do with this energy is transmute it from one form to another. Thoughts are nothing more than the movement of consciousness. **This is the law of consciousness.**

Law 2: Everything around you, seen and unseen, is connected through the same energy. The Hermetic saying "as above, so below; as within, so without" reflects this truth. Consider everything in life as its own field of energy that flows from one form to another but is never separate from everything else. **This is the law of relativity.**

Law 3: Everything in the world vibrates at a specific frequency. The frequency at which a thing vibrates gives it its unique properties. When everything appears to be still, it is in constant movement. Your thoughts are the primary vibrational cause of all the things around you. Your emotions have great energy, and of all the things you could feel, love is the most potent and fastest-acting vibration. On the other end of that spectrum is fear, the slowest energy. Your universe has 12 unique vibrational layers. Each dimension vibrates faster than the last and has less energetic density. Don't think of the dimensions as actual places but as frequency ranges. **This is the law of vibration.**

Law 4: As everything is in perpetual movement, a constant rhythm directs this movement. This rhythm continues eternally, causing patterns to repeat themselves as seasons, developmental stages, cycles, and so on. Think of everything that exists as a pendulum. If it swings to the left, it must swing to the right, and vice versa. The determining factor of this rhythm is consciousness. **This is the law of rhythm and cycles.**

Law 5: One all-powerful sovereign being oversees everything in existence, and there is none above it. This being is omnipresent and omniscient. It is consciousness itself, and since you are essentially consciousness expressing yourself as a human being, this implies there is no one above you. You are a sovereign, self-deterministic being with no leader governing you. There is no old, gray-bearded man in the sky, overlooking everything you do, preparing to give you a stern talking-to about your choices. You can lead your life responsibly, honoring all other lives around you. When you understand your sovereignty, you always act from a place of love and care for others. To recognize you're a sovereign being, know yourself. If you do not, you will find yourself constantly under the sway of other forces outside of you. Even then, realize that you are the one in power. You are so powerful that you have given yourself and those forces the illusion that they, not you, are in control. **This is the law of sovereignty.**

Law 6: Your thought is the first creation. Sound is the second creation responsible for creating the divine blueprint upon which your life is built. Light is the final creation that gives form and structure to all created things. Nothing that exists or will exist that is not already created energetically. If you can think about it, it is real. Of all created things, nature reigns supreme. The point of creation is to allow consciousness to come to know itself in every way possible. Consciousness is doing this every time through you and everyone else. **This is the law of creation.**

Law 7: All created things exist in duality. Polarity is the order of the day. In other words, everything must have its opposite form. But upon closer inspection, you'll realize that these opposites are the same thing but with differences in the degree of expression. The universe's power sources are rooted in the principle of polarity. The only way to experience what is up is by experiencing what is down. **This is the law of polarity.**

Law 8: There is only one time, and that time is now. There is only one place, and that place is here. You are now here. You are nowhere! And yet you are everywhere, all at once and simultaneously. Everything in the universe exists in the same space and time, but because of their different rates of vibration, you may not be able to perceive them. **This is the law of spacetime.**

Law 9: All energies that vibrate at the same frequency are drawn to each other. You have a saying on the planet that opposites attract, but this is not the case. In this universe, like attracts like. When you have two things that vibrate at different frequencies, they are naturally opposed to each other and will repel each other. **This is the law of attraction.**

Law 10: This is a universe in which free will is honored. You have the right to do whatever it is you like at any point in time. Even though, for the most part, humans tend to forget this and act like trees rooted to a particular position forever. You can do whatever you want as long as it is from a place of love. If your actions aren't rooted in love, that would be tantamount to enforcing your will upon others, and that is not going to work out very well for you because this is a universe of free will. **This is the law of free will.**

Law 11: All actions have an equal and opposite reaction regardless of what they are. Cause and effect are real and inescapable. This is karma! Whatever you dish out will be meted out to you in the same measure. This law is reminiscent of the law of attraction, where like attracts like. Never assume that there is such a thing as coincidence and randomness in your universe. Luck is not a thing. All causes have effects, and all effects have causes. All things are caused by consciousness, which is what you are. When you understand this, you will have mastered reality creation. **This is the law of cause and effect.**

Law 12: Consciousness takes energy and converts it into matter. The manifestation process is the result of working with these 12 laws. The world is set up so that when you follow these laws, you will get the results you seek in your life. **This is the law of manifestation.**

Why Pleiadian Wisdom Is Necessary for Pleiadian Starseeds and Society

Pleiadian wisdom is vital for Pleiadian Starseeds and society because working with this wisdom can allow the collective to transform and achieve its highest potential. Even on an individual level, following these laws and teachings will assist you with making your life the way you've always wanted it to be. Here is how Pleiadian teachings benefit you and society as a whole if followed:

Pleiadian wisdom is essential to bring the community closer together.[20]

1. *You will experience an awakening and an expansion of your consciousness.* As you study what the Pleiadians have to share with you, you will find it necessary for your soul to awaken to experience higher levels of consciousness. Do you realize that you could be so much more aware than you are right now? You can tap into your most authentic self and reach out to your higher self to fully express your spiritual potential. When you know who you are, the world you live in, and the connection everything has to one another, you will experience true peace and power.

2. *Pleiadian teachings are powerful for personal transformation.* The Pleiadians care about the acceleration of the evolution of the human collective. However, they're also concerned about your personal expression of your grand ideals. Studying Pleiadian wisdom will lead you down the path of choosing to be responsible for your choices and your life as a whole. This happens because the teachings awaken you to the power within you. The deeper you dive into them, the more you will discover the limiting beliefs that have kept you back from greatness. You will no longer be able to stumble through life unaware and blind to the patterns that have held you captive. This means that your newfound awareness will make it easy for you to break free and ascend to greater heights than you thought possible. You learn to heal and love yourself and turn to the power within. The more you do this, the better it will be for the collective.

3. *Pleiadian teachings uncover the secret of unconditional love.* Love, as humanity generally expresses it, seems to be shackled to one condition or another. Pleiadian wisdom is about teaching you how to live from your heart and embody love without shackles. You learn how to be more compassionate, how to express your love, and how to be understanding of everyone around you. This is a good thing because it means that you will be a vessel for peace and harmony on the planet to create a more compassionate society. When humanity embraces true, unconditional love, it will demonstrate phenomenal power that can allow humanity to become what it was destined to be.

4. *Pleiadian wisdom can help you get in touch with the cycles and energies of nature.* You'll come to learn that nature does have cycles. You'll discover that you are a part of nature and cannot escape those cycles. When you choose to go with the flow instead

of fighting your natural self, you will experience a fuller life. By following Pleiadian wisdom, you will learn how to live in alignment with natural energies like those from planetary alignments or moon phases to experience spiritual development and well-being. Also, you'll find yourself deeply connected to the Earth and the universe. This implies you'll find it easy to work with the universal laws and gain access to higher frequencies.

5. *Pleiadian teachings are essential for the awakening of the collective and for the transformation of the planet.* As a Pleiadian Starseed, it is your responsibility to embody your authentic self. You have so many unique gifts to offer the world. By educating yourself on the ways of the Pleiadians, you can begin to live in a way that demonstrates your awareness of the interconnectedness of everything. You'll find that when people come together with the same intentions and aligned actions, magic happens. Learning more about what the Pleiadians share helps you as a Starseed to awaken others.

How to Receive Messages from the Pleiadians

Before attempting to contact the Pleiadians, you have to understand certain things. First of all, it is possible to reach them externally *and* internally. External contact would involve actually meeting the extraterrestrials physically. This is not common, but it tends to happen in remote locations that don't have a lot of human traffic. Thankfully, the other, more accessible way to contact the Pleiadians is internal, through spirit or energy. The next thing you must do is shift your mentality on how these things work. There are seven things you need to keep in mind:

1. Always remember you're reaching out to Pleiadian Energy, not a person. Think of Pleiadians as a field of light in the fifth dimension. They can show up to you as a human with an angelic aura or as light. However, the Pleiadians do not have to embody specific forms. Try to loosen up your expectations about how your connection should play out.

2. Think of the Pleiadians as your family and not aliens. After all, as a Pleiadian Starseed, you are one of them. With this thinking, you stop assuming they are foreign to you and remove the feelings of fear or hostility.

3. Think of the process of connecting with Pleiadians as returning home. It's an unmistakable vibe you will recognize once you feel it.
4. Don't approach them with the idea of worshiping them. Remember, you are a sovereign being. Just because they understand things beyond your ken does not imply you should worship them as gods. Instead, love them.
5. Connect with your heart, not your head. Pleiadian energy is the kind that resonates with the soul. Do not expect them to connect with you on a mental level. Your brain's only function during channeling is to facilitate the connection with them on a heart level and interpret their message.
6. You do not have to leave your body before you connect with Pleiadians. As a matter of fact, they would prefer that you remain grounded instead of astral projecting.
7. Finally, remember that you are a Pleiadian. You may have chosen a different form and life, but that does not make you less Pleiadian than the Pleiadians with whom you wish to connect.

Now that's out of the way, the question to be answered is how to connect with them practically.

- Use meditation and mindfulness practices. Your mind must stay quiet as you connect to higher consciousnesses. For this to happen, you must practice meditation every day. As you sit in silence with your eyes closed and your attention on your breath, set an intention to connect with a Pleiadians. Using your feelings or heart, let them know they are welcome to show up. Also, keep an open mind to whatever may arise, whether visuals, insights, messages, etc.
- You can also connect to the Pleiadians using intuitive guidance. Your intuition is the language of the soul, and the Pleiadians will communicate with you on a soul level. To understand them better, check with your gut on all your affairs. Make working with your intuition a part of your lifestyle. This will help you improve at detecting the messages it has for you.
- Try automatic writing and channeling. When you meditate to the point of stillness in your mind, you may bring out a notepad and a pen and write whatever comes to you. Note that this process is

not forced. It should feel free-flowing. Alternatively, you may channel by allowing whatever words feel right to flow out of your mouth unimpeded. Ideally, work with a recorder so you do not forget what was shared.

- Make a practice of journaling your dreams. Sometimes if you can't get clear messages from the Pleiadians, they may reach out to you through the language of dreams. You can also deliberately intend to meet with them in your dreams. They will usually honor invitations. When you go to bed, ensure your dream journal and pen are right by your side, so you can note everything that transpired before you forget. Pay attention to symbols, messages, or themes that strike you. It's okay not to understand what the dream is about at first. But trust that the meaning will reveal itself in time.

- Make a point of noticing synchronicities in your life. Remember, there is no such thing as coincidence. If you notice that you keep hearing a word or seeing numbers at certain times, it could be the Pleiadians trying to reach out to you. Synchronicity can also play out as events, such as running into a specific animal or color over and over. Try to maintain an attitude of curiosity and fascination whenever you notice this happening, and it'll happen more and more. In due time, you can interpret what those synchronous events mean.

- Finally, make a daily practice of sacred rituals – and have a sacred space you use in your home. When you have a sacred space where you retire to perform your rituals, something about that encourages the presence of the Pleiadians to be even more pronounced in your life. Consider burning incense, lighting candles, working with crystals or tarot cards, or whatever resonates with you. Before you begin your rituals, set an intention to let the Pleiadians know that they are welcome. Here's a bonus tip: try working with lunar phases, planetary alignments, and other celestial events, as this can help you establish a stronger connection to these beings.

Criticisms and Controversies

Naturally, the Pleiadian teachings have some criticism and controversies surrounding them. The public is unwilling to entertain the possibility that other life forms than humans exist. Here are some of the most common points that attack Pleiadian teachings.

1. There is no scientific proof that Pleiadians exist. The many claims of Pleiadian contactees and channelers are often questioned and debunked because there's no scientific evidence. A counterargument to that criticism is you must realize that spiritual experiences and connection with extraterrestrial entities tend to be subjective experiences. This subjectivity means it is impossible for science as we know it today to investigate these phenomena. It is unfair to invalidate one's personal experience because it cannot be weighed against scientific measurements. Besides, science is still playing catch up regarding matters that spiritual people have known for thousands of years.

2. Some argue that the idea of Pleiadians and what they teach is all cultural appropriation, a distortion of various indigenous beliefs from different cultures. While this is an understandable criticism, a counterargument is that Pleiadian teachings seek not to exploit different cultures but offer guidance to allow people to grow and transform their lives. All religions have a piece of the truth. Pleiadian teachings are simply putting all the pieces together.

3. Those who ridicule the idea of Pleiadians claim that there is no consistency in their message and a lot of contradiction. This tends to happen because various people channel Pleiadian energy. Inevitably, channelers' interpretations will distort the message somehow, as they have their unique understandings of life, meaning there will be some discrepancies. However, it is undeniable that the Pleiadians are always about healing, love, and spiritual awakening, no matter whom the message comes through.

4. A final criticism is that skeptics think that Pleiadian wisdom is simply the commercialization of New Age ideas to extract financial profits from those gullible enough to believe extraterrestrials are real. It is tough to argue against the fact that there are unscrupulous individuals in the spiritual community who take advantage of others. However, these people do not negate the presence of genuine teachers and channels of the Pleiadian beings. Some channelers have integrity and want nothing more than to help humanity transform into its grandest,

best version of itself. It is a matter of discernment and paying attention to the message rather than the parts that can be sold for profit.

Being aliens, the Pleiadians have deep knowledge of the stars and the cosmos. Would you like to know their view on astrology and how it can help you grow and manifest the life of your dreams? Head on to the next chapter on Pleiadian astrology.

Chapter 4: Pleiadian Astrology

Possessors of Advanced Cosmic and Stellar Knowledge

The Pleiadians have an advanced knowledge of the stars and the cosmos.[21]

The Pleiadians are highly evolved beings. They possess a deep connection to the higher realms and advanced knowledge of the stars and the cosmos. They understand frequency, energy, and how planets interact with one another in their home star system. Pleiadians are multidimensional, meaning they exist in multiple dimensions simultaneously, ranging from

3D to 9D. Since their existence is so rich and layered, it implies that they have access to knowledge that is not yet available to humanity. One way to access this knowledge is through astrology.

Being cosmic travelers, the Pleiadians are particular about exploring the universe to its furthest reaches. As the Pleiadians travel, they learn valuable information about various civilizations, planets, and star systems. In other words, the Pleiadians are among the wisest beings in existence. Their wisdom extends to such things as astrology and stars in general. They can tell you better than anyone the way the various celestial bodies interact with one another, the effects of planetary alignments, and cosmic energies. You can use this information to guide your path through life, for divination, or to understand why your life is the way it is.

Astrology as a Tool to Access Pleiadian Knowledge

Pleiadian spiritual practitioners actively work with astrological events and alignments as tools to heal, grow spiritually, and manifest whatever they need. These events in the stars affect individuals and collective consciousness. It only makes sense to actively pursue a deep understanding of the workings of these events and learn about the stars from the Pleiadian point of view. Now, let's dive into details about how astrology can help you access Pleiadian wisdom.

Astrological events are tools to help with manifestation.[22]

1. *You can use astrology as guidance.* The Pleiadian perspective on astrology states that the celestial bodies' movements and energies can potentially serve as guidance. When you study the placements of the planets on your birth chart and the astrological configurations in your life, you gain insight into how these energies interact and affect your life. You will never be taken by surprise by whatever comes your way at any point in time.

2. *Astrology can help you understand soul connections better.* Pleiadians teach about soul contracts and soul connections. No soul on Earth or anywhere else exists in isolation. Everyone is related to everyone else in some way, and there are specific connections that have a purpose. When you examine synastry, which involves the side-by-side comparison of birth charts of different people, you can figure out the spiritual lessons you came here to learn from these connections with others.

3. *Astrology can help you understand the energetic patterns in your life.* Since every celestial body has a unique influence on how you live life, you can grasp the effects of the energetic patterns emitted by those bodies in terms of the challenges you have to go through and what you need to develop as a person. By studying the energetic patterns, you gain a better idea of where you can grow and what your strengths are. You also know how to take advantage of energies that could assist you along your spiritual path.

4. *Astrology offers an explanation of your evolution.* Life is meant to evolve, and as part of life, you actively have an evolutionary path to follow and a purpose to fulfill. By studying your birth chart and other astrological elements, you can discern what you came here to learn and experience in your life. You can use the configuration of the planets on your birth chart and at the present moment to guide you toward fulfilling your grand purpose and your soul's desire.

5. *Astrology helps with the appreciation of synchronicity.* Remember, there's no such thing as coincidence. Everything that happens in life does so at a divine time. When you consider astrological events like progressions and transits, you will notice that they reflect the presence of a higher form of intelligence. The more you study the interplay between these astrological events, the more you will understand the best time to seek growth and integrate lessons to manifest and transform your spiritual life.

The Effects of Astrological Events

First, consider *eclipses.* There are two kinds of eclipses: solar and lunar. Each of them is an extremely powerful event because they manifest portals of energy that you can use to transmute whatever you want in life. When the moon passes between the Sun and the Earth, that's a solar eclipse. However, when the Earth casts a shadow on the moon, that's a lunar eclipse. How can you take advantage of this astrological event? If there is anything in your life that you would like to change for the better, you can use the eclipse; simply integrate it into your spiritual practice by acknowledging the energy and drawing upon it using your words and intention.

The solar eclipse, in particular, is awesome for bringing forth the new and creating lasting major changes in your life. As for lunar eclipses, they are best for helping you work through your emotions. If you've been hurt and are struggling to heal, you should work with the lunar eclipse. This eclipse will help you let go of old ways of thinking and being so that you can finally be free of the pain you are experiencing. Both eclipses are excellent for achieving growth as a collective and on an individual level.

Retrogrades are also very powerful astronomical events of which you can take advantage. A retrograde is the seeming movement of a planet backward in the sky when viewed from Earth. Pleiadian astrology emphasizes that retrogrades are excellent periods for reflection and introspection. It's a great time to look within and reassess your choices so far. While eclipses are great for outer manifestation, retrogrades are perfect for inner work.

Humans tend to hide certain truths about themselves from themselves. Sometimes, this self-deceit is because they lack the courage or strength to face those truths. Other times it's because they assume there is something to be gained from ignoring the truth about who they are. Hiding from the truth about yourself can hold you back in life. So, use the retrogrades to help you discover the hidden parts of yourself. Realize that not all hidden truths are necessarily wrong or harmful. Within those truths are the kernels of strength and the manifestation of greatness beyond your dreams.

Another set of powerful astrological events is *planetary conjunctions.* Whenever at least two planets are closely aligned with the same zodiac sign or degree, that is considered a planetary conjunction. This event has the power to affect the collective and planetary energy. The effect of the conjunctions you're dealing with depends on the planets in question. For instance, in December 2020, Saturn and Jupiter were in conjunction, which was the catalyst for the start of a new cycle where there was a shift in social structures, aspirations, and beliefs. The cycle is set to last for the next 20 years.

You must also consider *outer planet transits*. Uranus, Neptune, and Pluto are considered outer planets. When in transit, they affect everyone and can last a long time. Uranus transits, for instance, tend to be disruptive. However, it's important not to view the disruption as terrible because within it lies the opportunity for you to set yourself free. Uranus transits are excellent for causing awakenings across the board. You can expect constant innovation and sudden change. Neptune transits are all about illusion and spirituality. You can expect to experience greater intuition when this planet is in transit. You'll find it easier to connect to your spiritual side. With Pluto transits, an intense, deep energy encourages change and leads to the destruction of old structures and systems. Keeping track of these transits allows you to take advantage of them.

The final astrological event you should note is a *planetary aspect*. Planetary aspects include oppositions, trines, squares, and conjunctions, and they all affect the human collective and the planet's energy. The best aspects that encourage the flow of creativity and cooperation are trines and conjunctions. On the other side of the table, you have oppositions and squares, which are aspects that lead to challenges and cause tension in your life. However, they are useful because they can lead to change, growth, and resolution for the better.

Practical Applications

Now that you know about astrological events, the next question naturally arises: How can you incorporate them into your spiritual life? Here are five different ways you can do so.

Set your intentions first thing in the morning. When you wake up, before you roll out of bed to start your day, take a moment to consider how you want your day to go. Obviously, you should already be aware of the astrological events taking place. This means you should have done your research the day before. For instance, if you're aware that there's about to be a powerful solar eclipse, you can set an intention to embrace a new start in your life, whether that's in your finances, love life, or something else. If it helps, you can say words out loud to invite your desired changes. Visualize the energy from the solar eclipse pouring into your body and flooding you from head to toe. Firmly state out loud that you are ready for and open to the changes to come.

Practice meditation and reflection regularly. Set a specific time every day for this practice. Having a dedicated space in your home for this purpose would also be helpful. Ensure you're wearing comfortable clothing and won't be distracted for at least the next 10 to 15 minutes. Sit or lie down comfortably, shut your eyes, and pay attention to your breath. When you feel that your mind is calmer and you're more present, turn your attention toward the cosmic energy of the astrological event in question. Visualize or feel this energy flowing through your body, and then bring to mind whatever it is you wish to reflect upon, change, or heal. With each breath, feel the energy growing more and more intense. After the meditation, you can write any insights you may have received in your journal during your mindfulness practice.

Use sacred practices and rituals to help you tap into the energy of the event. These practices don't have to be extremely complicated. You may have an altar at which you pray, or perhaps you enjoy having candles and incense while reflecting on the energy. Breathwork, chanting, and visualization are also valid practices to work with. Choosing practices and rituals that align with who you are is important. Also, keep an open mind because you may be inspired to try something different that will help you harness the energy even better than ever.

Get your creative juices flowing every day. Find time in your day to engage in creative activities where you can access and channel the energy of the astrological event. You could paint, write poetry, play music, dance, or engage in other creative pursuits. The point is that this activity should allow you to pour out your emotions. In your mind, find ways to incorporate your desires and the insights you've gained over time, and allow the energy to be your inspiration and guide during your creative process.

Have a mindfulness ritual that you perform before going to bed. It could be as simple as writing a gratitude list, choosing to be forgiving, letting go of any emotions that don't feel good, saying prayers or affirmations that align with the energies of the astrological events, and so on.

If you have any other ideas or inspirations about how you can work with these energies outside of these five suggestions, definitely use them. Whatever you settle on, it is important to make it a daily practice because the more you purposefully work with these energies, the easier it will be for them to flow and have actual perceivable effects in your life.

Astrological events undeniably impact your life. As Earth begins its journey from the age of Pisces to the age of Aquarius, it's crucial to understand the energies that are coming in, so you can work with them. But what does the age of Aquarius actually mean? Find out in the next chapter.

Chapter 5: Pleiadians and the Aquarian Age

The Age of Aquarius is an astrological concept. It signifies a time when the Earth's rotational axis, relative to the stars, undergoes a slow wobble, and the sun moves over a span of 2,160 years. The Earth's axis remains in constant motion, gradually shifting. As time passes, the vernal equinox traverses the different zodiac signs. Humanity is now entering the Age of Aquarius, supplanting the preceding Age of Pisces.

The Aquarian constellation.[23]

Themes of the Age of Aquarius

The Age of Aquarius has themes and characteristics that set it apart. The first is that of individualism and collective consciousness. You may have noticed that people are more focused on individuality. You may find yourself more interested in developing your freedom as a person. The energy of the age of Aquarius drives everyone to pay attention to what makes them unique and to express their authenticity. Interestingly it balances this focus on individualism by also encouraging a focus on the relationships between all people. This is a period when you can expect to see the elevation of collective consciousness to the point where humanity finally lives in unity.

The twin themes of social progress and humanitarianism also are the hallmark of the Age of Aquarius. At this time, people are strongly motivated to consider humanitarian values in their choices. Humanity is awakening to the fact that social progress is required, as for a long time, people have been living repressed lives. So there is now a focus on justice and equality and ensuring that every last person on earth has their basic needs met. This age is about building communities working with one another, with a singular goal of improving the state of humanity.

Another thing to notice about the Age of Aquarius is the rapid development of technology and constant innovation. If you've been closely observing humanity's journey in science and technology, it would appear that the race has made quantum leaps. Take a look at the world of artificial intelligence, for instance. Every day there is a new robot, ability, and AI modality enhancing life on Earth. Aquarius is under the influence of Uranus. The energy of this planet is all about revolution, innovation, and scientific progress. So it's only natural that there will be rapid development in science and technology. Humans will be even better at developing new ideas and identifying needs that weren't obvious. No one knows for sure what the next new thing will be. However, you can be sure it will affect how you communicate, interact and live.

The Age of Aquarius is also a time when consciousness will be elevated as people awaken spiritually. Those who have never considered the broader aspects of themselves will suddenly find that they're drawn to spirituality. Everyone is becoming more aware of an innate hunger to explore their soul. Where we once lived in a society primarily dominated by scientific, empirical facts that the five senses can observe, humanity is shifting toward exploring the esoteric world in as much detail as it has the physical. This will affect all aspects of life.

The Connection between the Age of Aquarius and Pleiadian Teachings

While there isn't necessarily a collectively agreed-upon correlation between the themes of Pleiadian teachings and the Age of Aquarius, undeniably, there are similarities to be found between them. For one thing, the Pleiadian message and the Age of Aquarius are about the collective shift in consciousness. They emphasize that there will be a transition from the old into the new. Pleiadians teach that humanity is going through a period of change where awareness becomes heightened, and the spiritual journey becomes more intense. This is the process of aligning with a higher purpose - something the Pleiadians continue to talk about in all their teachings. It is the awakening of humanity's spiritual nature.

Pleiadians also teach about the importance of elevating consciousness and promoting unity. As mentioned in previous chapters, these beings are aware of the interconnectedness of everything and everyone in existence. They realize that understanding this interconnection is critical to experiencing true love and unity in all realms of existence. These values are also encouraged by the Age of Aquarius' energy. This age will be all about moving beyond the ego's stories and limitations, allowing for a more robust expansive transcendent connection with one another.

Both the Pleiadian teachings and the Age of Aquarius are about spiritual awakening. Both embody the idea that humans will become way better at using their intuition and other psychic abilities than they already are. Pleiadians encourage people to get in touch with the wisdom within them. You have to learn to trust your intuition. You should also follow that fire within you that pushes you to learn about esoteric knowledge. You're not alone in this journey. The entire collective is waking up to the higher dimensional selves along with you.

Pleiadians are also about healing and universal love. Whenever channeled, they often ask people to learn to be compassionate towards themselves, others, and the world in which they dwell. These admonishments echo what is to be expected in the Age of Aquarius. The better you get at embodying love and emanating healing energy, the more positively the world will be affected.

Going through Pleiadian teachings, you'll find that they address the importance of spiritual guidance and assistance. These beings are ever present and ready to offer you the help you need on your spiritual journey. If you resonate with the teachings of Pleiadians — and you do, otherwise, why are you reading this? — realize that you have a vital role to play in the collective's shift during the Age of Aquarius.

Please remember that the connections between the Pleiadian messages and the Age of Aquarius are nuanced. The age of Aquarius is an astrological concept. Pleiadian teachings, on the other hand, are a result of channeled information. So you may find some disparity between various points of view on each of these concepts.

Pleiadians on DNA Activation in the Aquarius Age

The Pleiadians have spoken about the activation of dormant DNA in humans and the potential waiting to be unlocked in humanity. They teach about the DNA being an energetic blueprint that contains the template for awareness in multiple dimensions and accelerated growth, spiritually speaking.

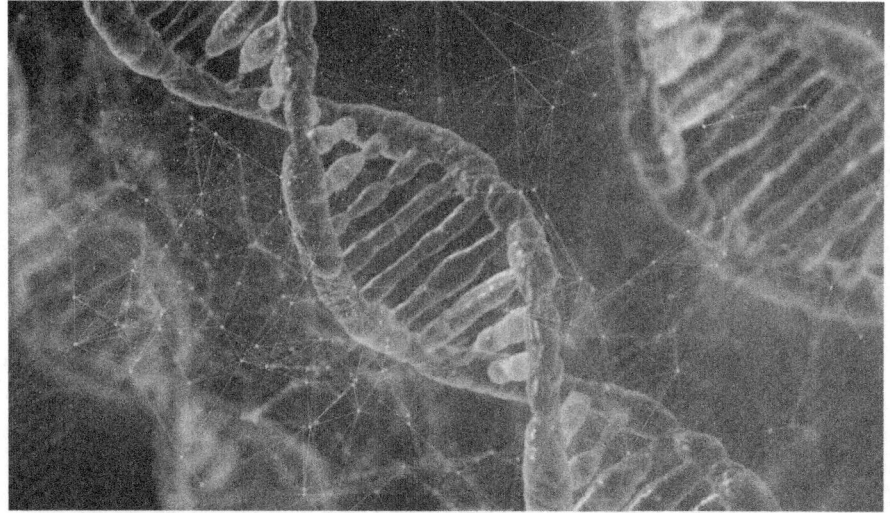

Pleiadians believe that humans have dormant DNA that needs activation.[34]

Cosmic energies and planetary alignments also have an effect on dormant DNA. How do you activate your dormant DNA? By using the power of the astrological events discussed earlier. By deliberately tapping into these energies and setting the intention to awaken what's asleep within, you will begin to experience phenomena that, once upon a time, people deemed impossible or the stuff of fairy tales.

DNA activation is essential for the awakening and evolution of the collective. This is why you should have a daily practice that aligns you with the higher frequency of the Age of Aquarius. You carry within you great wisdom from ancient times. Unlocking this wisdom can cause your awareness to expand, help you grow to spiritual maturity and even take your intuition to great heights. You will find a plethora of spiritual gifts. Whether it's healing, telepathy, channeling, intuition, expanded perception, the awareness of multiple dimensions, or connection to higher realms, activating your DNA will give you all this and more.

Do the work to create the best conditions that allow your DNA to activate. This means practicing self-reflection, learning about energies, making meditation a daily practice, ensuring you speak your truth, and so on. When you choose to live consciously, you obliterate all energetic obstructions that keep you from expressing the powers locked within you.

Pleiadians teach that DNA activation is not something that happens in a vacuum. Practice collaboration and appropriation with everyone on the planet. So, while you do your bit to access the powers within you, collaborate with others to share what you know and what you've experienced so they can learn from you and grow, too. Also, if your heart is in helping the collective, you should integrate the energies of planetary events into your daily life. Find ways to insert this energy into every interaction that you have. You may not necessarily be talking about Pleiadians or other esoteric things. However, infuse that energy into your conversations as you interact with others. Let it flow from you when spending time together or even kicking around a ball, as this will cause your energy to rub off on them and draw them up to a higher frequency.

Note that what the Pleiadians teach isn't about having superpowers that you can flex with. It's not about showing off. It is about using those powers to help the people around you. When your heart is in the right place, you know these gifts have been given to you so you can serve others, the earth, and the cosmos. In the next chapter, you will discover whether you're a Starseed. How? With your birth chart.

Chapter 6: Starseed Birth Charts

What Is a Birth Chart?

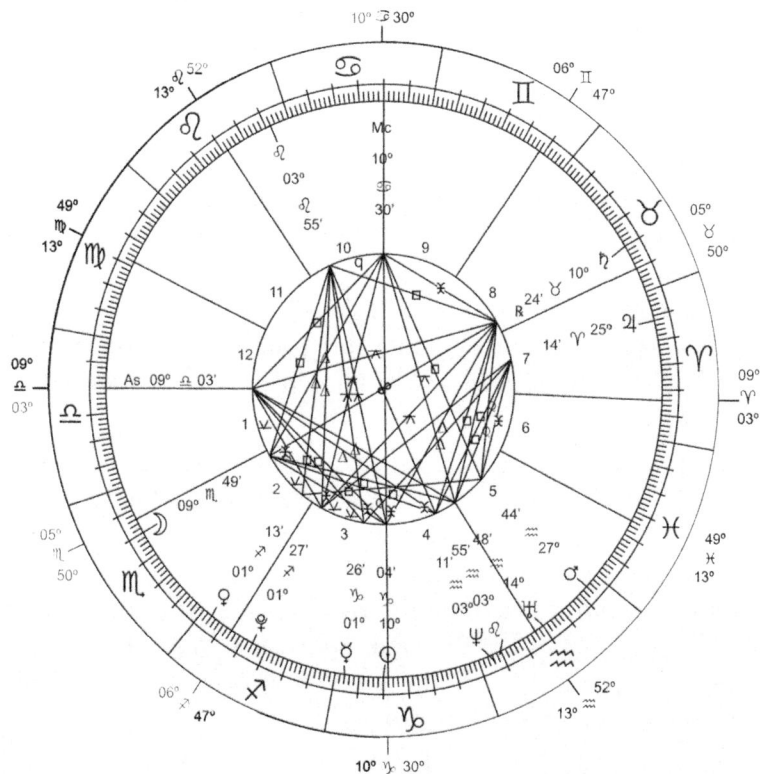

Sample birth chart.[25]

Your birth chart is also called a natal chart. It offers an overview of the planetary positions when you were born. Think of it as a snapshot of the celestial energies that were influential when you incarnated on the Earth. You can expect to find the Sun, Moon, planets, and other heavenly bodies on your natal chart. You must know when and where you were born to create your chart. It's also helpful to have the precise time of your birth.

The birth chart has several essential components that make it possible for you to interpret it accurately. First, the planets on your natal chart are representative of the various energies and archetypes of your personality and experiences in life. The astrological planets are the Sun, Moon, Mercury, Venus, Mars, Jupiter, Saturn, Uranus, Neptune, and Pluto. Each has its unique energy signature that affects you in different ways.

Your birth chart also has houses on it. These houses represent various aspects of your life where the planets' energies manifest. There are 12 houses on your chart. Each is connected to specific themes. The first house is the House of Self. It reflects how you appear. It's the first impression people get of you when they meet you. The next house is the House of Value. It involves your personal finance and things you own and hold in high esteem. If you want to know the state of your finances and how secure and stable you are, this is the house to check out.

The third house is the House of Communication, which represents thinking, learning, and how you interact with others. The fourth house is the House of Home and Family. This house represents home, family, and where you put down roots. This house tells you a lot about your emotional stability. The fifth house is the House of Pleasure, which is all about your romance, creativity, kids, and ability to express yourself fully. The sixth house is the House of Health, which is about the state of your well-being and how you work.

The seventh house is also known as the House of Partnership, which is representative of the relationships, marriage, and partnerships you may have in your life. It is about cooperating with others and finding harmony and balance. The eighth house is the House of Transformation. This house is about rebirth, death, and change. The House of Philosophy, or the ninth house, is about higher education. It is also about traveling to learn about new cultures, traditions, and philosophies. This house covers everything regarding personal growth and expansion.

At number 10, you have the House of Career, which is all about your reputation, social status, and work. It's about your ambition, drive, and the achievements for which you are recognized. The eleventh house is also called the House of Friendship. It represents the groups and social causes to which you belong. No one exists as an island. Therefore, this house is important because it allows you to find fulfillment in the best way possible, depending on what your birth chart says. Finally, there's the twelfth house, the House of the Unconscious. It represents everything connected to your unconscious or subconscious mind, karma, and spirituality. This is the house of introspection. It invites you to look within, grow spiritually, and transform your life.

In addition to planets and houses, you will find zodiac signs on your natal chart. There are 12 zodiac signs, and they all have different traits and qualities. The 12 zodiac signs and sequential order are Aries, Taurus, Gemini, Cancer, Virgo, Libra, Scorpio, Sagittarius, Capricorn, Aquarius, and Pisces. Your Sun sign is the one that the Sun was in when you were born.

Aspects are another vital part of the natal chart. Aspects are the angular relationships between all the planets on your natal chart. They tell you a lot about how the different energies from different planets interact with one another and affect your life. The main aspects on your chart are the conjunction opposition trying square and sextile. Conjunctions are what you get when planets are close to each other. Opposition aspects on your birth chart occur when two planets are on opposite sides. You have a trine when two planets are 120 degrees apart, a square when they're 90 degrees apart, and a sextile when they are 60 degrees apart. Together, they let you know the challenges you may experience and your potential.

Why Birth Charts Are Necessary for Finding Your Starseed Origin

Your birth chart is essential as it helps you figure out your Starseed origins and understand your soul's journey. A critical look at your chart will let you know which energy signatures and indicators are present and help you pinpoint your Starseed origins. Among the indicators that help you figure out where you're from are planetary realignments, aspects, star systems that show up on the chart, and, most importantly, the nodes. Remember, when the planets are in particular positions and certain aspects show up in your chart, they could line up with energy frequencies from a star system or more, which will give you a clue about your Starseed origins.

Curious about the astrological factors that are important in determining your origins? Well, the first thing you need to consider is the planetary alignments. Next, you must look at the nodes of the moon. You see, the North and South nodes of the moon are vital when figuring out what your past life was like and what your present life's sole mission is. You must also consider the star systems and fixed stars on your chart. For instance, Arcturus, Sirius, Orion, or the Pleiades are all connected to Starseed origins, and if they are prominent on your chart, this could mean that you are tied to those places on a cosmic level.

Pleiadians emphasize the importance of exploring your natal chart to understand your true nature and what you are capable of. The Pleiadians teach that your soul will pick a particular time, date, and place of birth to take advantage of the available planetary energies to develop and grow. Your natal chart will teach you everything about the lessons you're supposed to learn in this life. If you're feeling lost and unaware of your talents, you can use your chart to figure out what you should do with your time and energy. Working with the information you get from your natal chart is a great way to accelerate your awakening and spiritual development. Also, understanding your natal chart will not give you an easy breezy life, but it will make your challenges less daunting since you already know what you'll be struggling with and where your strengths lie.

Interpreting Birth Charts with Pleiadian Influences

When interpreting your natal chart, you must look at certain aspects and other factors strongly connected to Pleiadian frequencies. First, consider what's going on with the Pleiadian cluster on your chart, particularly concerning the personal planets. The Sun, Moon, Mercury, Venus, and Mars are considered personal planets, and when they are in conjunction or close alignment with the Seven Sisters on your chart, this tells you that you are very likely Pleiadian.

Another interesting fact about Pleiadian Starseeds is that they are strongly Venusian in their energy. Remember, these beings are all about beauty, harmonious living, and love. These traits are reflective of the planet Venus. If you have Venus in Libra or Taurus, you have Pleiadian origins.

If you are a Pleiadian Starseed, the odds are you have major planetary placements in the fifth house or the seventh house. Remember, the fifth house is the house of creativity and self-expression, while the seventh house is about relationships send partnerships. As a Pleiadian Starseed, it is natural for you to desire to express yourself creatively and connect with others.

A final sign to look out for on your natal chart is whether you have positive aspects connected to Neptune. You see, Neptune is a planet that encourages spiritual connection. It is about realms higher than Earth. Neptune is also the planet of intuition, and as a Pleiadian Starseed, you may have positive aspects like trines or conjunctions between Neptune and other planets. If you do, you can connect to spiritual wisdom and access the guidance of the Pleiadians.

The Importance of Nodes

Pleiadians teach that the North node is a powerful sign of your soul's path and Starseed origins. If your North node is in Libra or Taurus, you are strongly connected to the Pleiadians because those zodiac signs possess powerful Pleiadian energies of harmony, love, and spiritual development.

The South node represents your past life and the patterns of karma you contend with. If you are Pleiadian in origin, you may notice that your South node is an Aries or Scorpio, and this could be a sign that you struggle with being assertive, transforming yourself, and dealing with power dynamics. When you choose to work through these obstacles, you can finally become much higher in frequency, emanating even more Pleiadian energy than you already do.

You need to pay attention to the nodal aspects. These aspects are between other planets and your North and South nodes, and they can tell you more about your Starseed origin story and your soul's evolution. Harmonious aspects like sextiles or trines between the Moon, Neptune, or Venus and your nodes could be signs that you are Pleiadian.

Assume that you're looking at a natal chart and realize that your Sun lies in conjunction with The Pleiades cluster. That would mean the energies of the Pleiades highly influence your fundamental self. It suggests that your purpose for being here on earth is to express wisdom, love, and spiritual growth. If Venus lines up with the Pleiades, you are drawn to beauty, harmony, and love. Therefore, whether it's your relationship, creativity, art, or aesthetics, you are highly influenced by Pleiadian energy.

What if your chart has a harmonious aspect between Neptune and the Moon? What this means is that your intuition is off the charts. And not only that, you are in touch with your emotions. To develop spiritually, you must rely on your intuition and emotional sensitivity. Now, assume that on this same natal chart, you find that Pluto and Mars form a challenging aspect. This would imply that you must find a way to change your assertive energies and balance them out. Other astrological elements that demonstrate Pleiadian influences include:

- A cluster of planets in Cancer, Gemini, or Taurus
- The moon in Pisces or Cancer
- Venus in Libra or Taurus
- Neptune in a prominent position on your natal chart
- The North node is positioned and cancer Gemini or Taurus
- Harmonious aspects with the midheaven or ascendant

If you want more information on identifying your Pleiadian roots, head to the next chapter.

Chapter 7: Identifying Your Pleiadian Origins

How to Discover Your Pleiadian Roots

Identifying your Pleiadian roots requires self-discovery and being in touch with your intuition.[96]

Do you want to discover your Pleiadian roots? Well, you should remember that this journey is very personal. It requires you to be in touch with your intuition. While you can learn a lot from astrology, the fact remains that true self-discovery is something you must do by going within.

Let's look at five possible ways to dive deep and explore your Pleiadian roots without needing external influences to help you.

First, you must practice self-reflection: Make it a daily habit to reflect on your day and how life has been lately. Meditation, journaling, and mindfulness are helpful practices for self-reflection, and they'll help you to pay attention to the whispers that come from within you. Sit in stillness, and you'll notice your intuitive thoughts bubbling to the surface for you to address and acknowledge.

Decide to become a seeker of knowledge and wisdom: Take a deep plunge into the vast sea of Pleiadian wisdom, so you can learn everything you can about the mythology surrounding the Seven Sisters. Search the internet or your local library for everything connected to the Pleiades or Pleiadian energy. The more knowledge you soak in, the faster you awaken to who you really are and the wisdom you carry within you.

Connect directly to the Pleiadian energies: By practicing visualization exercises, you become attuned to the Pleiadian frequencies. You can also invite them to be present during the most mundane events of your everyday life. By accepting and acknowledging that they have heard you, you will naturally draw them close to you, and this will help you learn more about your Pleiadian roots. You may experience dreams or out-of-body projections during which you discover truths about your Pleiadian ancestry.

Respect the gift that is your intuition: You must learn to trust the wisdom that comes from within you. Intuition, when split into two different words (in-tuition), is literally "teaching that comes from within." As a Pleiadian Starseed, you have the Pleiadian energy within you, and it contains all that you require to know about your past and future as a constantly evolving soul. So, notice when you find symbols that pop up repeatedly in your dreams. Pay attention to synchronistic events, as these could be guides showing you the path you need to walk.

Find your tribe: You have to look for other people who are just like you. Find people who are just as passionate about learning about their Pleiadian ancestry. Suppose it's tough to find people around you interested in esoteric knowledge. In that case, you may use the internet to find fora, social groups, and local gatherings near you. Build a community of people who share the same values as you do, as this will accelerate your ascension as a soul. You will have more information about who you are as a Pleiadian Starseed.

Signs That You Are Awakening as a Pleiadian

You have chosen to walk the path of awakening. This means you will never be the same again. To be successful on your journey, you must stay open and continue to reflect on your life and your choices. You must have a strong desire to know who you are and be willing to plumb the depths of your soul. As you embark on this personal, highly spiritual journey, you will begin to experience signs that you are waking up as a Pleiadian. Awakening plays out differently for everyone, and the insights you gain will differ from what the next person gets. Having said that, here are some potential signs to look out for:

Your sensitivity levels increase significantly: As you begin to realize who you are as a Pleiadian and accept your origins, you will find that you are increasingly sensitive to emotions, energy, and any subtle changes or vibrations in your immediate environment. Increased sensitivity gives your life experience depth, allowing you to truly understand where you are at every point. You become much more aware of your emotions. Usually, people walk around like zombies, unaware of what causes them to shift from emotional highs to emotional lows. However, awakening as a Pleiadian means you will recognize these shifts as they begin. This implies that you'll discover patterns of behavior that do not serve you and preempt them before they can take hold in your life, as they've always done. Being increasingly sensitive is beneficial because it helps you become more empathetic toward others. You learn to notice what you can see, hear, *and* feel. This way, you can interact with others from a place of power, safety, and love.

Your consciousness will expand: As you awaken to your Pleiadian origins and integrate them, you will find that your perception of reality will blossom. You begin to question the nature of existence, realizing that the conventional way of doing things does not seem sustainable. You think about deep topics like the true nature of reality and the point of life. You consider the connection between spiritual and material existence. As you work on expanding your consciousness, you will feel a pull towards looking at different religious ways of thinking, philosophies, and other practices that could shed light on the truth of existence. You also find that you are no longer a victim of dualistic thinking, where you assume that it's either black or white. You start to see the shades of gray in everything, understanding that life should be viewed from a more holistic point of view. Your expanding consciousness implies you will have access to such depths of awareness you could never have imagined before you began your journey. You may discover psychic abilities or even extrasensory perception, which will help you access wisdom unavailable to most.

Your intuitive abilities will be activated: The deeper you dive into your cosmic roots, the more you will find your intuitive gifts becoming obvious. For one thing, you will get clear messages from your higher self. These messages can show up in various ways. You may have dreams, receive flashes of insight during meditation, or even experience direct communication through automatic writing or channeling. You have internal knowing without being able to explain how you know what you know. As you dive into your Pleiadian origins, give attention to the intuitive nudges you get because they will play a role along your journey. You may find it unsettling, at first, how intuitively on the mark you are. But give it some time, and you'll get used to it. It does not matter how silly the nudge appears to be. If you get an inclination to stand by your favorite coffee shop at 2:13 pm, you should do that without asking questions. These intuitive nudges matter because they will bring you the opportunities and experiences you need to grow.

Challenges the Awakened Pleiadian Will Face

As you become more aware of who you are as a Pleiadian and Starseed, you must remember that you will encounter a fair bit of challenge. You may see these challenges as obstacles, but that's not the case. You can use them as stepping stones or fuel for the fire that burns within you to transform yourself and humanity for the better. Without further ado, here are some of the challenges that you will encounter:

You may initially feel overwhelmed by the process of integrating your multidimensional awareness. An inevitable side effect of awakening to your Pleiadian origins means that you will expand your awareness far beyond what is typical for humans. You will receive information and sensations from dimensions besides the physical one. As a result, this may be challenging to handle because you will be barraged with too much information. At least, that's what it will feel like at first until you get used to it. Your relationships will take a hit as you attempt to balance your new expanded consciousness and regular mundane life. You should find a way to maintain harmony with the people around you and stay grounded while being aware of other realms.

You may experience uncertainty as you figure out your belief systems. There is no way to avoid the process of shifting your beliefs as you accept that you are a Pleiadian. Many beliefs you hold near and dear will be challenged. This is not easy, as many people identify with established thought patterns. Trying to suggest that the things they buy into are inaccurate and unnecessary can feel like an eradication of the individual. You must go through this process. You'll find yourself letting go of the conditioning you have accepted and been programmed with from birth. You'll release the programming from parents, authority figures, religion, culture, society, the media, etc. As you shed the limiting beliefs that do not serve you like dead weight, you become lighter, evolving into a light being as you honor your truth, which will bubble naturally from within you. Beware, however, of the temptation to suggest to others that their beliefs are invalid. Those who would awaken by observing the changes in your life will do so naturally. There's no need to force your beliefs down anyone's throat.

The emotional turbulence as a result of your healing may be uncomfortable. Waking up means you will begin to feel emotions on a deep level as you heal all the damage from living a life of less consciousness than you're experiencing. You will notice that past wounds and traumas begin to resurface in your conscious mind, asking to be resolved. Patterns that have plagued your ancestry for generations will surface, seeking to be released and healed. You must understand that this process is rather intense. You must be courageous and stand firm because gold must pass through intense fire to be purified. You are gold. Be kind to yourself as you experience this process. You need to seek out a community that understands what you're going through. Take care of yourself. Don't skip a day of mindfulness practices. Also, do not attempt to repress any of these traumas because that will only cause your discomfort to increase and last longer.

You may experience resistance and fear as you discover your true purpose. Realizing that you're here to serve humanity and heal the planet can feel like a lot. It's understandable to want to shy away from such a huge responsibility. However, you must remember that you are not alone in this process. You are not like the mythical Atlas saddled with the world on your shoulders with no one to help you carry it. You have an entire family that spans generations and across the globe working on the same goal. So do not be afraid to lend your passions, unique gifts, and insights to the cause. Be unafraid to step into the shoes of your true self because this is part of your evolution. It is inevitable, so you might as well enjoy the ride and embrace it fully.

You may have trouble balancing your spiritual and material lives. You're becoming aware of higher frequencies. As a result, you will be exposed to uncommon phenomena and lines of thought. Some people get a little too lost in the source and forget they must do basic things like continue their career path, keep their relationships thriving, and take care of daily responsibilities. Deal with this challenge by staying grounded in reality while you experience your spiritual evolution. You can do this by taking the spiritual insights you get from your practices and integrating them into your everyday activities.

There will be challenges to face when it comes to handling your energetic sensitivities. You cannot avoid becoming more sensitive to your environment, so you'll pick up other people's energies and emotional states. Sometimes it's almost as if you can read their minds. If you're undiscerning, you may assume someone else's thoughts are yours. The way to handle this challenge is to learn to set up energetic boundaries. You must cultivate practices that help you become more aware of your true self. You already know mindfulness is an excellent tool to help you with this. Working with acupuncture, pranic healing, meditation, or Reiki is also effective. If you find yourself completely overwhelmed by someone's energy, you can practice energetic cord-cutting. Visualize energetic cords connected to you and this person, and then imagine them being gently cut and dissolved into nothing. You can also envision yourself surrounded by a white or pink bubble of light so that you do not take on other people's energy as you go about your day.

You may find this journey rather lonely and alienating. When you don't have people around you who share the same Pleiadian ideals, you can feel as if you're alone in the world. You yearn to be understood, but sadly, it's a rare soul who will get you. This is why you must proactively seek like-minded people and build a community that supports you. Go for spiritual gatherings, and check out online fora to meet others and form a family.

You'll have to do some shadow work and practice self-integration. As a Pleiadian Starseed who was awakened, you can't skip the work required to heal the parts of you that you have continued to deny or ignore. You must bring your shadow to the light so that not only can you heal, but you can integrate the gifts that lie within the shadow. Many assume the shadow self is horrible and has nothing good to offer. They believe the shadow should therefore be repressed. However, your shadow houses some of the most profound things about you. This is because your shadow is composed of all the things that people did not approve of and that you willingly rejected so that you could fit in. Remember that, as a Pleiadian Starseed, you must be authentic. So, shadow work is not optional. To help you along your journey, you can work with healers, therapists, and spiritual guides to integrate this aspect of yourself and become whole.

You'll start to remember past life memories that you have to integrate. As you awaken to your Pleiadian roots, you may recall events from your past lives. This recollection can happen as flashes in your mind. Alternatively, you may experience those lives in your dreams. Discovering that you used to be a cold-blooded Roman commander who loved war a little too much can be very jarring. Imagine finding out that you've lived lives where your present values are the antithesis of those past characters you once played.

In other words, the experience of recalling and integrating these memories is intense. You must be patient with yourself and practice discernment to avoid taking on qualities from those lives that would not serve you. Also, it would be helpful if you worked with therapists or spiritual guides experienced with past life regression therapy. Journaling and meditating are excellent tools to help you integrate these memories in an empowering way that enriches your present life experience.

You may be tempted to shy away from awakening, but you must not. These challenges are an invitation you should accept to grow beyond who you are and do something far more beautiful. Trust that you will be supported throughout your journey. Embrace everything that comes with it with an open heart and a willingness to go beyond your present limitations, regardless of how that would look.

Traits and Characteristics of Pleiadian Starseeds

There's an erroneous assumption that Pleiadians have physical characteristics or markings that set them apart. Please note that this is not the case and only fuels unnecessary discrimination and division among people. Pleiadians are thought of as having pale skin and light blue eyes. While this is the case for their original form, that does not imply that only humans with the same traits can be or are Pleiadian.

Remember that as a Starseed, you are a reincarnated soul. That means you can be born into anybody of any skin color, form, or gender. There are, however, certain traits that set you apart as clearly Pleiadian. These character traits have already been clearly addressed in Chapter 2, so you can refer to that if you'd like a refresher.

So, you now recognize that you are a Pleiadian Starseed. Are you curious about how the Pleiadians communicate? The next chapter will teach you everything you need to know about the Pleiadian light language and how to activate it.

Chapter 8: Pleiadian Light Language

What Is Pleiadian Light Language?

Cosmic light language carries all the wisdom of different cosmic entities and galactic civilizations."

The Pleiadians have a language that is no respecter of barriers in terms of dimensions. It is far above and beyond anything written or spoken in the history of humanity. This language can break past all communication barriers because of its vibrational nature. As you already know, everything in life moves and vibrates. This means that this language is easy to understand for one and all and is powerful at effecting change when used for that purpose. This language has encoded messages, energetic activations, and frequencies that bring healing and transformation. This is the Pleiadian light language.

Properties of Light Language

Pleiadian language works with the principle of vibration. Everything that exists is energy; therefore, it is easy for the Pleiadian light language to affect one and all. Every symbol, tone, and sound of this language is calibrated to frequencies that have unmistakable effects on the energetic structures of environments, objects, and people.

Pleiadian light languages work with special symbols known as sacred geometry. Some people hear the term "sacred geometry" and assume it's a square or a circle blessed with holy water or something, but that's not the case. The shapes of sacred geometry are the building blocks of all creation. These shapes are the basic principles and patterns that power reality.

Sacred geometry are thought to be the building blocks of creation.[28]

For instance, you have the Flower of Life, a pattern with circles overlapping one another and representing the energy of unity and creation. Then there's the vesica piscis, with circles intersecting, carrying within it the twin energies of interconnection and divine balance. Sacred geometric shapes are essential as they hold energetic frequencies and information. These shapes transmit activating, healing, and transformative frequencies.

Since the Pleiadian light language is rooted in sacred geometry, it can break through all limitations of conventional language and interact directly with you on a multi-dimensional level. The encoding present in the language is responsible for the dormant DNA activation to put you in touch with your higher self. This allows you to evolve spiritually and awaken to heal yourself on all levels. As you work with this language, you'll be able to awaken parts of you that have been asleep and unconscious for a while. You'll find yourself becoming more creative and expressive. You'll easily accept wisdom, guidance, and support from higher-dimensional entities.

If you're struggling with energetic blocks, need an effective way to balance your chakras, heal your emotional trauma, and so on, the Pleiadian light language is excellent for helping you achieve all this and more. This is because this language realigns you with your highest purpose. With it, you can eliminate all the fluff to cut through to the true essence of your being. There are many ways in which you can express Pleiadian light language. You could create art with it. You could write it or speak it. And just like conventional language, you can sing it.

Types of Light Languages

There are several different kinds of light languages with their unique characteristics and uses. They've been categorized in various ways, but you must understand that these categorizations are not necessarily rigid and are subjective in interpretation. Here are some of the most common Pleiadian light languages that you may encounter:

Galactic light language: This light language is tethered to Pleiadian teachings and comes from the Seven Sisters. It can be expressed vibrationally in different ways, including symbols, energetic codes, tones, sounds, etc. This form of light language transcends all other languages, with effects so far-reaching that they affect the entire cosmos.

Angelic light language: This language is specifically for the angelic realms and is used by angels. Its frequencies are of divine guidance, healing, and love, and often it sounds melodious. This language is spoken with movement that is graceful and harmonious. With this language, we'll be able to connect with angels, receive angelic energies, and channel angelic messages. It is also an excellent language to use when you seek the assistance of these divine beings.

Cosmic light language: This form of light language transcends specific realms. It carries all the wisdom of different cosmic entities and galactic civilizations. It is used to transmit cosmic codes and higher-level knowledge that allow consciousness to evolve.

Elemental light language: Elemental light language is connected to the realms of the elements and the consciousness of the different spirits that inhabit nature. When speaking this language, you will need gestures, symbols, and sounds to properly channel the energies of the elements you're dealing with. Gestures help to establish a deep, strong connection to the world of nature. This language brings balance and harmony to your environment and encourages elemental beings to work with you for good.

Soul language: This variant of light language is the expression of your soul's essence. It communicates your soul's frequencies and the purpose for which you exist. This language is authentic. It requires intuitive communication and deep awareness of your truth. You can use this light language to help you with the alignment of your soul and discover more about who you are that you have not yet learned. Use this form of light language to help you tap into your gifts and the wisdom you carry.

The Process of Pleiadian Light Language Activation

To activate light languages, you must be able to send and receive the frequencies in alignment with Pleiadian energy. Your experience may differ from someone else's. The following is a description of how the process usually goes.

First, is the awakening. Deep within your soul, you experience a longing to connect with realms beyond the physical. For inexplicable reasons, you desire to grow spiritually and learn as much as you can about the worlds beyond Earth. You may also find yourself becoming more interested in the stars, and in your heart, you will sense that there is much more to your life than you currently know.

Next comes your alignment and the clearing of energies. As you answer the call to awaken, you find yourself experiencing alignment and energetic clearing. In other words, your past limiting beliefs, old patterns of behavior, and emotional blocks that keep energy from flowing within you are eradicated. If you want to accelerate this process, you should consciously set the intention to do so. Be open to having healing energy flow through you. Meditation will help you with this step.

Next, you will experience a conscious connection with the Pleiadians. As you maintain your daily spiritual practices like meditation, visualization, and so on, you will inevitably open yourself up to Pleiadian energies. To encourage them to show up for you, intend to connect with them. Perform invocation rituals so that they know you are ready for their wisdom, frequencies, and energy activation. You must ensure that you come from a place of love and not fear as you do this.

Next, you will receive activation codes and downloads from the Pleiadians. These codes and energetic downloads could come as intuitive knowing or symbols. You may not be able to interpret the information within them in human language. Still, on a deep level, you will sense that you understand what you're looking at. That is because these energetic downloads and activation codes connect directly with dormant parts of you. They directly affect the higher-dimensional aspect of your being so that you can expand in consciousness.

Now it's time for practice and integration. At this point, you should learn how to allow the energy to flow through you and be expressed in whichever way feels natural. You may be drawn to pick up a paintbrush and create art. You may find yourself singing or chanting during meditation, writing automatically, or simply speaking. At this point in the process, do not allow your conscious mind to talk you out of continuing. The Pleiadian light language activation process is beyond logic, so do not try to cage the process with logical, rational thought. It is a language of the soul.

You must understand that the process of Pleiadian light activation is not something that happens once and is done. It is a never-ending journey where you continue to dive deeper into consciousness and gain more insights and energetic shifts along the way. Make a point of nurturing your connection to the Pleiadian energies, and you will expand in ways you never thought possible. This expansion is awe-inspiring and necessary for all of humanity. It is your duty, and you should not shy away from it. Instead, be thankful that you get to be part of such a great and noble cause.

Benefits of Pleiadian Light Language Activation

Pleiadian light language activation benefits you in multiple dimensions. After activation, you'll experience amazing effects on your life, and your spiritual journey will be accelerated beyond the imagination. One of the benefits of Pleiadian Light Language activation is that your consciousness will expand, and you'll access higher dimensional states of awareness and have a deeper understanding of how everything in the cosmos is connected. This will do wonders for your manifestation abilities and help you feel more love and compassion for others and yourself.

The Pleiadian light language is also an excellent tool for energetic healing. As you work with this language, you will find that the symbols, codes, and frequencies it carries will help you become whole. Since the odds are you must have experienced traumatic events at a young age as a Pleiadian Starseed, this language can help you integrate those events and heal from the wounds that they left you with. Also, by working with this language to bring balance to your chakra system, you will experience better health mentally, physically, and spiritually.

Another benefit of Pleiadian light language activation is that it allows you to connect with your spirit guides. You were never meant to go through life alone. You were never meant to live in complete confusion, feeling lost all the time about what to do next with yourself. Light language is an excellent tool to help you gain the spiritual guidance all humans are entitled to. No matter what situation you're faced with, you will receive the best counsel about how to handle it. As you act on the messages you receive, you'll find yourself trusting your guides more, and this will only lead to you becoming more open to higher dimensional energies. In other words, the more you trust, the more you are trusted by a higher intelligence.

Pleiadian light language activation allows you to express yourself powerfully and to become more confident in who you are. This is because it inevitably strips you of the superficial so you can be more authentic in expressing yourself. As you work with Pleiadian light language, you'll find that you eliminate all forms of self-doubt. When you communicate with others, you speak from a position of power and love that is difficult to ignore and always leaves everyone listening blessed in some way. Something about the light language activation makes it easier for you to share your truths and bless others with your gifts. As you know, this is a good thing for the collective awakening.

By working with Pleiadian light language, you will constantly upgrade your frequency and activate the necessary DNA to become more than who you are. On top of that, you will find that your life feels more harmonious and balanced than ever. Since light language activation balances your body's energetic centers, you will experience harmony in mind, body, and spirit. This inevitably will lead you to connect with other dimensions of yourself. As a result, you will experience a life of peace, clarity, and a great sense of well-being.

Preparing for Pleiadian Light Language Activation

The days and weeks before you experience your Pleiadian light language activation, you must take steps to prepare for the process. Here's a walk-through of what you must do:

Take time to set the intention for light language activation and to self-reflect. Be clear on what you hope to gain from the experience, and affirm that you're ready to receive the energies.

Do some inner work and energy clearing. After self-reflection, emotional or energetic blocks which won't serve you should surface. Set the intention to clear these blocks. Journal to get all the emotions you feel out of you. Seek a therapist if you can, and don't neglect the act of meditation. Clear stagnant energy and negative emotions to create a receptive environment for the Pleiadian energy to flow through you and allow light language activation.

Practice energetic hygiene. This means you need to be mindful of the kind of media that you consume at this time. Also, beware of the thoughts you entertain. Do visualization exercises where you clear your energy and cleanse your aura. Also, ensure that you are grounded.

Spend time in nature. You can walk around the park barefoot if you can swing it. Nature has energies that help you ground yourself and stay aligned with your authentic self. When you achieve this alignment, it will be easier for you to connect with the Pleiadian frequencies.

Do work to expand your consciousness. This means meditation, mindfulness practices, and breathwork. These help you remain grounded and present. Remember that you will not be able to receive the Pleiadian light language activation if you do not know how to root yourself in the here and now.

Work with affirmations and visualization exercises. Using visualization, you can imagine that you are already connected to the Pleiadian frequencies and have experienced the activation. Imagine these experiences as having taken place in your past because that makes it easier for you to accept that it is a done deal. Affirmations are also excellent for programming your mind to prepare for the activation. Affirm that you are ready and at peace with whatever the process will look like.

Take good care of yourself. Engage only in activities that will feed your mind, body, and spirit with good energy. You could practice yoga or Tai Chi, go for energy healing sessions, and make a point of remaining in a state of relaxation and joy.

Finally, you must be in a state of surrender and trust. Trust that the activation will happen when it should, neither later nor earlier. Surrender to the process however it unfolds for you. This means you need to let go of any expectations you may have from reading or learning about someone else's activation story. Do not be overly attached to specific outcomes so that you do not feel disappointed if it doesn't play out that way. Also, realize that being attached to outcomes makes it almost impossible for you to experience the Pleiadian light language activation.

Now you know what to do to prepare for this event. It's time to look at the steps to activate the Pleiadian light language in your life.

1. Set up a sacred space that is quiet and free of distractions. You can make the energy of that space positive by lighting incense, smudging it, or lighting candles.

2. Ground and center yourself to develop a strong foundation energetically speaking. To do this, close your eyes, take deep breaths, and imagine roots extending from your feet into the ground. Seated in a lotus position? Imagine the roots connecting your buttocks to the Earth. Notice red or white energy flowing up from the Earth into you, making you feel rooted and secure.

3. Set your intentions. Ensure that they are clear. Think about what you plan to gain from the experience. Do you want guidance, healing, or for your consciousness to expand? Get clear and be

bold about setting these intentions.

4. Visualize all stagnant negative energies acting as energetic blocks within your body and mind flowing out of you through the roots beneath you into the Earth. As you do this, make sure you continue to breathe deeply, and with each exhale, imagine your body becoming lighter and more flexible. Do this long enough, and you will begin to sense pure, vibrant energy flowing through you.

5. Open up your energetic portals. Envision a column of white light that flows from the sky through the top of your head or your crown chakra, moving all the way down through the other chakras until it terminates at the root chakra.

6. Now, it's time to connect to the Pleiadian energies. Visualize a beam of loving white light or a sphere that encompasses you. This light is the Pleiadian energy. Stay open to all the gifts that they have for you as you feel this light moving through you and around you.

7. Verbally invoke the presence of the Pleiadians. Let them know you're thankful that they're here to help you. You may allow yourself to smile if you wish because this will raise your frequency and make it easier for them to start the process.

8. Let the Pleiadian light language flow through your body and mind. Trust what's going on without having any resistance or judgment about what you're feeling. If you sense you should move your body in a certain way, allow your body to flow. If you get the urge to begin singing, speaking, chanting, or whatever else, go with it. Surrender to whatever is going on in the moment.

9. You can tell when the activation is finished because you sense a feeling of completion. At this point, you need to take some time to integrate your experience. You may have received insights or felt a shift within you. Revisit the experience in your mind, and express your gratitude to the Pleiadians. Thank your higher self for its role in the process because it helped facilitate the light language activation process.

Please note that you can make any changes you desire to this process. Above all else, you should always follow what your intuition leads you to do.

Using Sound and Movement

As you've probably deduced, working with your chakras is essential to activating light language. Each of the energy centers you carry has a specific sound that can be used to activate it. The following are the seed syllables of each chakra:

Working with chakras is needed to activate light language.[29]

Root Chakra (Muladhara)
Seed Syllable: "LAM"
Pronounced: "lahm"

Sacral Chakra (Svadhisthana)
Seed Syllable: "VAM"
Pronounced: "vahm"

Solar Plexus Chakra (Manipura)
Seed Syllable: "RAM"
Pronounced: "rahm"

Heart Chakra (Anahata)
Seed Syllable: "YAM"
Pronounced: "yahm"

Throat Chakra (Vishuddha)
Seed Syllable: "HAM"
Pronounced: "hahm"

Third Eye Chakra (Ajna)
Seed Syllable: "OM" or "AUM"
Pronounced: "ohm" or "aum"

Crown Chakra (Sahasrara)
Seed Syllable: "NG" or "OM"
Pronounced: "ng" or "ohm"

As for movement, you can make use of hand mudras. These are specific positions in which you hold your hands and fingers to allow energy to flow through your body. Here are mudras you can use for each chakra.

Root Chakra (Muladhara)
Mudra: Prithvi

Hand and Finger Placement: Put the tip of your ring finger against that of your thumb, and extend the other fingers.

Effects: This will stimulate your root chakra and keep you grounded. It also reduces anxiety and helps you feel more confident.

Sacral Chakra (Svadhisthana)
Mudra: Varuna

Hand and Finger Placement: touch the tips of your little finger and thumb to each other while the other fingers remain extended.

Effects: This mudra is connected to the water element. It will awaken your sacral chakra, help you become more creative, and give you better control of your emotions. It is also excellent to help you attract abundance and boost your well-being.

Solar Plexus Chakra (Manipura)
Mudra: Agni

Hand and Finger Placement: Press the tip of your middle finger into your thumb at the base. Bend your thumb over your middle finger to touch your ring and middle fingers while the index finger remains extended.

Effects: You'll awaken your solar plexus chakra and ignite your inner fire. This is great for digestion, faster metabolism, increased energy, willpower, confidence, and inner strength.

Heart Chakra (Anahata)

Mudra: Hridaya

Hand and Finger Placement: Bring the tips of your middle and index fingers and thumbs together while the other fingers remain extended.

Effects: This mudra is called the "heart seal." It will help you restore balance to your heart chakra. Using it, you'll feel harmony, compassion, and love. You'll also find it easier to heal and forgive.

Throat Chakra (Vishuddha)

Mudra: Matangi

Hand and Finger Placement: Interlock your fingers with both hands and put your left thumb over your right. Extend your middle fingers, pressing them together as they point to the sky.

Effects: This mudra wakes your throat chakra, making you better at expressing yourself, communicating with others, and being creative. It can help you speak honestly and clearly, and bring harmony to your mind.

Third Eye Chakra (Ajna)

Mudra: Hakini

Hand and Finger Placement: Put your fingertips together on both hands, with your palms facing each other. Your fingers should be extended, facing up, and with some distance between them.

Effects: This mudra will help open your third eye and give your insight, intuition, and concentration. You can do this when you meditate and want to go deeper. It offers you inner wisdom and opens the gates to higher consciousness.

Crown Chakra (Sahasrara)

Mudra: Shunya

Hand and Finger Placement: Bend your middle finger and press the tip against your thumb at the bottom. The other fingers must stay extended.

Effects: Shunya will activate your crown chakra, making you more connected to spiritual worlds. You will be more aware and experience life from a transcendent perspective. Use this to quiet your mind, and help you be more receptive to Pleiadian guidance. This mudra makes you at one with the universe and assists your spiritual awakening.

A final note: Don't be surprised if you feel the inclination to dance. Allow yourself to move freely. If you allow the energy to flow, the odds are your movements will be graceful and fluid, just as the Pleiadians are.

Now, how would you like to be able to connect with an actual Pleiadian guide? If you're not sure where to start, don't worry. The next chapter will show you how to do that.

Chapter 9: Connecting with a Pleiadian Guide

Your Pleiadian Guide

As a Pleiadian Starseed, you definitely have a Pleiadian guide. Generally speaking, the Pleiadians have a strong affinity for humanity. On an individual level, Pleiadian Starseeds have guides to help them along their life journey and spiritual evolution. Your Pleiadian watcher is all-wise and benevolent, and to have a proper connection with them, you must understand the role they are here to play in your life.

Pleiadian guide is a spiritual mentor.[30]

First, your Pleiadian guide is a spiritual mentor who works with you to offer you all the support and guidance you need. There will inevitably be times when you're at a loss for what to do about a situation. It is for times like these that your guide is present. Guides have made it their sole mission to help you with your evolution and awakening. The wonderful thing about them is that they offer you a much higher and broader view of life, spirituality, and what your soul is here to accomplish. More often than not, your guide knows you better than you know yourself. This is a great thing because they can offer you a deeper understanding of why you're going through the challenges you are facing and the paths you can use to overcome them.

Pleiadian guides are known to offer emotional and energetic support. Now and then, life will rock you with something so traumatizing that you experience emotional blocks. You find you're not quite able to access the universal energies with ease as you used to. Your Pleiadian guide can assist whenever everything is upside down, and nothing is going your way. They have the advantage of seeing just where you're blocked (energetically) and how you can get rid of that block. When you involve your guide in every aspect of your life, you will live a harmonious and balanced life.

Expanding your consciousness and awakening to your spiritual side is no easy feat; you will need help. There is no better being who can offer this assistance than your Pleiadian guide. Your guide ensures you can raise your vibration and access higher levels of awareness. They will do this by helping you unlock your spiritual potential that has lain dormant all this time.

Your Pleiadian guide also ensures you experience healing on every level and will lead you towards energetic and emotional practices that help you return to being whole. This healing and wholeness are necessary for you to express your highest potential.

If you're confused about your life's purpose or what soul contracts you may be involved in, your Pleiadian guide can assist you. You can ask your guide to reveal valuable insights from your past lives. If you like, they can help you understand the karmic connections that you have at present, as well as the lessons that you must learn and the experiences that you have chosen for yourself as a soul. Your guides can also help you develop a deeper connection to the higher realms. They can help you develop better intuition and other spiritual gifts, so it is easier for you to connect with the divine.

You may have wondered why you end up in certain difficult situations if you are supposed to have a guide always looking out for you. Keep in mind that the Pleiadians will always respect your free will. They'll never infringe on your personal choices. The best they can do is offer you support and guidance through your intuition, but if you ignore that guidance, the consequences are on you.

Remember that every Starseed's relationship with their guide isn't cookie-cutter; do not expect your experiences to mirror someone else's. If you want to take advantage of everything that comes with having a relationship with your Pleiadian guide, you must stay open to them. You must trust them fully and implicitly and do all you can to engage with them. This chapter provides guidance on how you can foster that relationship.

Creating a Sacred Space

Creating a sacred space to connect with your Pleiadian guide is vital. When you have a sacred space, the odds of deepening your connection to this entity and getting its guidance increase dramatically. Think of the sacred space as a container that separates your practice from every other mundane thing. So, whenever you enter your sacred space, you leave behind all non-essential thoughts and energies that could distract you from the task. This way, you can align with your Pleiadian guide and get the best out of your session with them. The following are some suggestions for creating a sacred space for your spiritual practice.

Pick a location. Your sacred space could be outdoors or indoors. All that matters is that it is somewhere that is comfortable, private, and has no distractions. You also want it to be a part of the room that you deeply resonate with. Maybe it's just a corner, the center of a garden, or an altar you've set up. When you choose this place, you should only use it for your spiritual practice. This way, you can continue building the energy so that it's stronger. You also program your subconscious mind to be more receptive to your guide's messages.

Now, it's time to cleanse and clear the place. Just because you've chosen a spot doesn't mean that is all that is required to get rid of any lingering energy that may not serve you, and that is why you practice energetic clearing and cleansing. You can spray the place with saltwater or smudge with Palo Santo or sage. You can also use singing bowls and ring bells to help clear and cleanse the energy. It is also important that whenever you want to use this space, cleanse your energy, too. This means letting go of any negative emotions or troubling thoughts bothering you. It's also good practice to take a salt bath, sage yourself, or meditate first.

Set your intention for your sacred space. Your intention should be your desire to connect with your Pleiadian guide and receive whatever you most need. Visualize your intention as an energy that is love and light.

If you don't already have one, build an altar. It doesn't have to be complicated, nor is it necessary. The altar could be a shelf, table, or some area where you can set up objects that matter to you or that resonate with your Pleiadian energy work. You can put candles, pictures of saints, symbols, mandalas, crystals, or whatever you want on your altar. Some excellent crystals you may want to work with to draw on Pleiadian energy include labradorite, blue quartz, and amethyst.

Incorporate all the elements in your sacred space. The four classical elements are earth, air, fire, and water. You can have a little potted plant, salt, or soil to draw the energy of the earth element. Use incense to represent the air element. A lit candle brings the fire element to play. Finally, a small bowl of water on your altar or anywhere else in your sacred space will bring the energy of water.

Place Pleiadian symbols and art around you. It could be a simple picture of the Seven Sisters or other Pleiadian symbology with which you resonate. Also, think about the ambiance and lighting of your sacred space. You might want to keep it soft, so that means using candles. LED lights are okay, too, if they can create the ambiance you seek.

Make your offerings. You could offer anything meaningful to you to show the Pleiadian guide you're dedicated to developing your relationship with them. Your offering could be anything from flowers and prayers to crystals and food.

Now that you have your sacred space, you must keep it safe, clean, and undisturbed. Remember that the purpose of this place is to deepen your connection, cultivate energy, and have your guide show up for you prominently every day. Have respect for the sacred space. Use it daily to intensify the positive Pleiadian energy and affect your life positively and profoundly.

Guided Visualization Exercises

In this section, you'll learn five guided visualization exercises that can help you connect with your Pleiadian guide.

1. **The Journey of Heavenly Unity:** After meditating for 5 to 10 minutes, notice how your mind is quieter. With your eyes shut, imagine yourself standing in a meadow. This meadow is so lush. Overhead is the night sky like a starry canopy. In your mind's eye, notice the Pleiadian sisters as they hang above you. Notice the warm glow of their energy. Now imagine that from the Seven Sisters, a celestial beam of light comes down. This light moves all around. It passes through you, and then it becomes a sphere around you. Allow the light to lift you off the meadow grounds and then to the air. Let it lift you higher until you float before the seven sisters in all their glory. Now notice your body gradually fading and becoming a light instead, just like the light surrounding you. Allow your light energy to merge with that from the Pleiades until you are one with it.

2. **Peaceful Etheric Gardens:** Imagine walking into an ethereal garden with every flower imaginable. All the flowers bloom brilliantly. The landscape before you is nothing but beautiful. It all looks so serene and calms you. As you stand in the garden, notice the gentle breeze that blows. Realize that this breeze is nothing more than Pleiadian energy. This breeze carries Pleiadian love and wisdom. Feel the breeze moving around you for as long as you want. When you're ready, start a conversation with your guide. Let them know your concerns, and trust that you will receive an answer either then or later.

3. **The Pathways of Awakening:** Imagine you are on a celestial pathway of gold, diamonds, and shimmering stars. As you walk up each step, you recall the feeling of being with your Pleiadian family. Feel the joy of reuniting with a long-lost one as you ascend these steps. At the top of the stairs is a being of light. This is your Pleiadian guide. Make your way up to them with love in your heart, and when you get to the final step, greet them with a warm hug. Tell them everything you'd like, then give them a warm smile as you end the conversation and thank them.

4. **The Cosmic Temple:** For this exercise, imagine walking into a sacred temple. This temple glows with iridescent light. You notice light patterns playing in the air as you enter the temple. Imagine these lights moving around you and through you filling you with a deep sense of peace. Continue walking through the temple until you come across a special chamber. This chamber

belongs to your Pleiadian guide. Make your way into the sanctuary paying attention to the beautiful symbols and sacred geometry around you. Now sit with your guide and commune with them with energy or words.

5. **Luminescent Ascension:** Imagine yourself being wrapped up in a cocoon of light. This light is like liquid gold, but it glows like the stars. Feel your body getting more relaxed as you lounge in this cocoon. Notice how your awareness expands, taking up more space than your physical body can. Now, imagine that your Pleiadian guide walks up to you full of light. You can feel the love vibrating from them to you. Imagine your guide extending their hand to you. You put yours in theirs. With a surge of energy, you push through into the heavenly realms together. As you journey through the stars, you feel transformative power flowing from your guide to you. You see it as light from their palm moving into yours, radiating through your entire body. This life is full of love, wisdom, and insight that you can use in your waking life.

By working with these guided visualizations, you will find it easy to connect with your Pleiadian guide. You can receive all the guidance that you desire from them. Just ensure that before you begin these exercises, you have a calm mind and are in your sacred space.

Other Meditation Techniques

Mantra Meditation and Breathwork

1. Begin by sitting in a comfortable position. It's helpful to have comfortable clothes on as well. Bring your attention to your breath.
2. Inhale. When you exhale, you can repeat a mantra related to your intention to connect to your Pleiadian guide. An example of a mantra could be, "I am open" or "I am ready."
3. Keep your attention on your breath and your mantra to help you quiet your mind so that you can be in the proper state to receive communication from your Pleiadian guide.
4. As thoughts come to your mind (and they will), notice that you've been distracted, and then gently release the thoughts. Do not beat yourself up for constantly getting distracted. Instead, be glad you noticed, then gently turn your attention back to your breath and the mantra.

5. Continue this meditation for as long as it's comfortable, and keep an open mind for any guidance or insights that may come to you.

Body Scanning

1. First, lie down or sit comfortably and then shut your eyes.
2. Bring your attention to your breath. Inhale and exhale as deeply as you can to relax your body. Shift your awareness to the here and now.
3. Begin with the top of your head to scan your body. You're going to work your way down to your toes.
4. As you pay attention to each part of your body, notice if there's any tightness or tension, and then take a deep inhale. On the exhale, release the tension in that body part. You may need to do this a few times before you move on to the next part of your body. The deeper you can relax, the easier it will be to receive the messages meant for you. Therefore, do not be afraid to return to your head and begin the relaxation process again as soon as you are done with your toes.
5. When your body feels completely relaxed, in your mind's eye, see a column of light flowing from the base of your spine up through the top of your head.
6. Notice that as the light shoots out the top of your head, it connects with the higher energies in the sky above you.
7. Keep your attention on this connection that you have created, and using your words or intention, ask your Pleiadian guide to be present.

Establishing a Connection through Sound

1. You may put on some soothing music if you wish. A quick search on the internet should show you playlists that are excellent for attracting Pleiadian energy.
2. Lie down or sit comfortably.
3. Shut your eyes and pay attention to the music. Let the sound fill you and help you attune to the higher vibrations of the Seven Sisters.
4. As you listen to the sound, utter an intention to connect with your guide. Feel love and appreciation for them because you know they will show up.

5. Whenever thoughts or distractions arise, notice that you've been distracted. Return your attention to the music and the feeling of love and appreciation.

Meditating with Nature

1. Find someplace serene and peaceful outdoors. It could be the beach, garden, or anywhere else.
2. Take a seat or walk around leisurely as you take in the beauty of your environment.
3. Notice how the connection between you and the natural world intensifies the longer you're there. This is good because the Pleiadians are also connected with nature's wisdom and harmony.
4. Continue to take in the peace of your environment as you ask for your Pleiadian guide to join you. Be open to your guide choosing to communicate with you through nature itself.
5. While you're there, keep an open mind to any symbols or intuitive insights that may arise within you as you sit or walk around in meditation.

All of these will work best if you maintain an open mind. Your intentions to establish a link with your guide should come from the heart, and you must show sincerity. Please know it might take some time and practice before you connect to your guide. However, that does not mean that your daily exercises are not working. You must be patient and keep at it.

Using Pendulums

A pendulum is an excellent tool for connecting to your Pleiadian guide and communicating with them. Wondering what a pendulum is? It's a small, weighted object hanging from a string or a chain. Holding the pendulum by the chain, you can swing the object back and forth or in circles. The pendulum is a divination tool that has been used for centuries and is considered reliable. The great thing about the pendulum is it helps you connect to your intuition and the higher dimensional energies around you. Without further ado, here's how to use the pendulum to communicate with your Pleiadian guide.

First, you must choose a pendulum. You could go to a new age or arts and crafts store. Or you can make one yourself if you'd like. What's important is choosing materials that resonate with you and Pleiadian energy. You'll have to connect with your pendulum, so you can't just pick the first one you find (unless it's the "one"). When you have the right one in your hands, you will know it.

Next, you must make your intentions clear. Before using your pendulum, ensure you know what you want to accomplish. In this case, you want to reach out to your Pleiadian guide. So, take a few moments to focus on that intention.

Now that your intention is set, it is time to energize and cleanse your pendulum. Your pendulum may have been handled by so many people before, so it is important to remove their energies so they don't interfere with your practice. How do you cleanse and energize your pendulum? Use sage to smudge it, put it in the moonlight, or put crystals around it.

It's time to calibrate your pendulum. You can't just start using a pendulum right away. Establish which directions it swings in when it says "yes," "no," and "maybe." First, hold the pendulum string or chain between your index finger and thumb. This should allow the weight on the other end to swing freely. Keep your hand steady, and notice what the pendulum does when it is neutral. Next, ask it questions that obviously have yes answers. Notice the direction in which it swings when it answers your yes questions. Then ask it questions that obviously have "no" as an answer. Note the direction of the swing. Finally, ask questions that have ambiguous answers. This step matters because it's how you figure out what your pendulum is telling you or what your guide tells you using your pendulum later on.

Ask yes or no questions. After calibrating your pendulum and spending some time in meditation in your sacred space, it is time to ask your guide some questions. Begin with questions that are straightforward to answer so that you can use them as a baseline to connect with your guide. You may ask your guide these questions out loud or in your mind. It doesn't matter.

You've got to interpret the responses from your pendulum. Notice the patterns, direction, and speed at which your pendulum swings. As you ask questions, you must ensure you tap into your intuition and trust it fully. The more you rely on your intuition as you interpret the responses, the more accurate your interpretations will be.

Keep your focus. You must stay grounded during the entire process. Now is not the time to worry about other things in your life. Stay calm and grounded. Suppose you feel like you're losing control of a session. In that case, all you need to do is pause and breathe in and out deeply, envisioning red roots coming up from the ground beneath you and connecting to your body. Envision all the nervous energy like a black, smoky substance flowing down through those roots into the earth. Let the smoke leave you for good, feeling calmer.

Offer your thanks and release the energy. When you're done communicating with your Pleiadian guide, it's time to thank them for their help. After thanking them, let go of the energy connection you have established through your pendulum.

Never forget that your pendulum is a tool that allows you to connect with your inner knowing and higher guidance, and it is no replacement for your intuition. It's only meant to help you to connect to your Pleiadian guide. So, you must practice discernment as you interpret the messages coming through. Also, the more you practice working with your pendulum, the more accurate the answers will be.

Using Oracle Cards

1. Choose a deck of Oracle cards. You could go for a deck that has Pleiadian imagery if you can find it.
2. Set your intention. What kind of messages would you like to receive from your guide? Say your intention aloud, or fix it in your mind.
3. Shuffle the cards. While shuffling, be gentle about it and keep your attention on your intention. Imagine your intention as a white light flowing through the palms of your hands and into the cards. As you do this, say a quick prayer to invite your Pleiadian guide.
4. When you're ready, draw a card. You must ensure that you are in touch with your intuition as you do this. If it helps, you can pick a specific card drawing method. For instance, you can spread out the cards in a fan or a straight line and draw the one that calls to you.
5. Now, look over the card and observe the imagery on it. If it has sacred geometry or text, consider what that means. Reflect on the connection between what you want to learn and what you see on the card. Trust your intuition as thoughts arise in your mind.

6. Whip out your journal and write down your experience. Note everything concerning your interpretation of the card and the sensations, emotions, and thoughts that surfaced while working with them. Journaling is good because it allows you to integrate what you've discovered instead of forgetting about it. So, resist the temptation to skip this step.
7. You can draw another card if you need further clarification on any topic. Draw as many cards as you need to get clarity. Remember, it's not just about picking the cards but focusing on them and seeing what your intuition reveals.
8. Finally, reflect on everything you've learned and figure out how to apply those lessons practically to your daily life.

Using Crystals

Crystals are an effective tool that you can use to amplify Pleiadian connections. To connect with your guide, consider working with these gems. Here's a step-by-step process that you can use:

1. First, select your crystals. Ideally, choose crystals that radiate Pleiadian energy. The best crystals to use for energy work include clear quartz, amethyst, celestite, lapis lazuli, and blue kyanite. If your intuition leads you to other stones besides the ones on this list, feel free to incorporate them.
2. Next, you have to energize and cleanse your crystals. To ensure their energy is pure, you should run them underwater to eliminate residual energy from other people that may not serve your purposes. Alternatively, you could smudge your crystals with Palo Santo or sage. When you're done, you can charge your crystals in the moonlight or sunlight or by burying them in the earth overnight. You can also hold them in your hands, set your intention to recharge your crystals, and envision that energy flowing through your palms and into your crystals.
3. Next, you must infuse these crystals with Pleiadian energy. You can ask your guide to help you with this process. Alternatively, imagine the Seven Sisters beaming light straight into the crystals before you.
4. Now it's time to meditate with your crystals in your sacred space. You can put the crystals on your body or hold them in your hands. If you put them on your body, you can place them over

the various chakra centers. Close your eyes and begin to breathe deeply to relax. As you float deeper into relaxation, imagine that the energy of the Pleiades is filling you, loving you, and supporting you.

5. Open up your heart and mind to receive all the messages from the Pleiadian realm of existence. Notice any sensations, images, or insights that flash in your mind as you meditate. As always, maintain an attitude of trust and openness.

6. Finally, it's time for you to express your gratitude and integrate your experience. Thank your guide for coming through once more, and then take some time to journal everything that you experienced and noticed during your practice. Integration also involves thinking about ways to take what you've learned and make it practical in your daily life.

Do you want to get better at contacting your Pleiadian guide using crystals? Practice regularly. When you stay consistent with it, you will only increase your proficiency and your connection to the Pleiadian energies with time.

Intentional Channeling

Intentional channeling is staying open to messages from higher dimensional beings. Many people assume that channeling is the same as being possessed, but that's not the case, as you are in charge of your body throughout the process. The following are steps to take to practice intentional channeling.

1. Set up your sacred space with crystals, candles, good music, and whatever else you need. Make sure there is nothing that would distract from your task.

2. Now you must ground and center yourself to ensure you have a powerful connection to the energies of the Pleiadian guides. If you want to ground yourself, breathe deeply and envision roots that come from your feet or buttocks and go into the Earth. You can also imagine a beam of light that shoots from the top of your head into the sky, connecting to the Seven Sisters.

3. Now it's time to set your intention as clearly as you can. Declare that you are ready to receive clear communication from your guide. State that you want these messages to be for your greatest good.

4. Now it's time to draw upon divine protection and light. Are there other entities you're used to working with? You can call upon them to be a part of the process. Ask them to be present and protect you from the energy that may seek to hijack the channeling process. It also helps to imagine a sphere of golden light around you that keeps every form of evil and no vibrational energy at bay.
5. Now it's time to meditate. Allow your body to relax and your mind to quieten as you do. Use whatever meditation technique works for you. Ideally, you want to feel your awareness expanding outward. As it expands, you will become more open to the higher energies around you.
6. The next step is to keep an open mind and heart as you connect to your Pleiadian guide. Ask whatever questions you may have. Share your concerns or intentions. You should surrender and be fully open so their presence and wisdom can flow through you. You must be patient with yourself and them and have implicit trust in the process.
7. Notice the images, words, symbols, feelings, and impressions coming up for you as you channel this energy. If you need to express their messages through spoken word, do so. Just make sure you have a recording device capturing everything you're saying. You may also prefer to allow the information to flow through you using automatic writing. In this case, you should have a pen and notepad ready and allow your hand to move however it feels. No matter how confusing or abstract the messages seem, this is not the time to try to analyze them. You can do your analysis when you're done with your channeling. As you listen to or read through what you have written or spoken, make sure that you take note of the insights and look for ways to ground them in reality.
8. Now it is time to offer thanks to your Pleiadian guide for showing up and answering your questions. Thank them for their constant presence and love in your life, and then end the energetic session with gratitude.

You have now mastered the various processes to connect with your Pleiadian guide. Well, now what? The evolution of your soul is not just for selfish purposes. You have the task of becoming a light worker. But what is light work all about? You'll find out about all that and more in the final chapter of this book.

Chapter 10: Healing and Lightwork

What Is Lightworking?

Lightworking is about intentionally bringing positivity, healing, and love to everyone.[31]

Everyone could use some love and positivity in their lives. The Earth sorely needs these things. Lightworking is about intentionally bringing positive change, healing, and love to one and all. The lightworkers are the people who chose to be born on Earth because they had the purpose of spreading light. They're here to raise the collective consciousness of the planet. You are a lightworker if you are a Pleiadian Starseed, for sure. You have to learn how to work with spiritual energies and other tools to help others awaken just as you have.

With your Pleiadian ancestry, you are responsible for helping the Pleiadian mission of bringing wisdom, love, and light to all beings on Earth. There are many ways in which your job as a lightworker can help the cause of spiritual development. First, not only are you to awaken and expand your awareness, you must help others do the same. Lightworking is a process that allows you to draw from the infinite well of spiritual gifts that lie within you. With these gifts, you help others around you to grow and heal from the trauma that keeps them stuck in debilitating patterns.

As you know, healing and change are Pleiadian themes and unavoidable when doing lightwork. You are an agent of transformation. Your job is not only to ascend on your personal spiritual journey but to help others do the same so that the planet itself can finally evolve into what it's meant to be.

Another spiritually significant thing about lightworking as a Pleiadian Starseed is that you get to spread compassion and love to one and all. The more you radiate these qualities, the easier it will be for others around you to emulate you so that their vibrations can rise, too. By choosing to be the example of compassion and love, you make it easier for others to create harmonious relationships and, ultimately, the best, most loving communities.

You, as a lightworker, have the mission to serve as an anchor for higher vibrations and frequencies to flow freely on the Earth. The more you acknowledge your role as a lightworker and do your best to embody that, the easier it'll be for the collective consciousness to rise. This implies the Earth will be full of unity, love, and spiritual growth.

Inevitably, you, dear lightworker, will be a part of the co-creation of the new Earth. Look around you, and it's clear that the Earth is indeed due for an overhaul. Your job is to work alongside the Pleiadians to create a new paradigm of awareness and consciousness that leads to more enlightenment on Terra.

While it's all nice and good to manifest a new house, a loving relationship, and an excellent career, you have an even greater calling. You are here to ensure that the new Earth manifests. This new Earth is rooted in harmony, peace, love, and spiritual evolution. This is how spiritually important your role as a lightworker is.

Characteristics of Pleiadian Lightworking

Love and compassion are the chief characteristics of Pleiadian lightworking. As a Pleiadian lightworker, you will feel a deep awareness of love and compassion within your heart. Everywhere you go, the unconditional love that radiates from you is unmistakable. This is because after your awakening and as you experience spiritual growth, realize that every being is connected to one another. Therefore, you send forth love in everything you do. Whatever you say, whatever choices you make, all of them spring from a place of love. You are intentional. You plant a seed of love in every heart you encounter.

Being a Pleiadian lightworker implies that you have some skill or mastery regarding healing and energetic affairs. It's not weird if you're naturally drawn to chakra balancing, reiki, or other energy modalities for healing and restoration. Healing energy flows through you unimpeded, and people can often feel this.

As a lightworker, you are also strongly connected to your intuition. There's never a moment when you can't access higher divine guidance. You know you can always lean on your intuition because you are sure you can trust yourself. You tend to receive deep insights, messages, and guidance from the Pleiadian realm and other higher-dimensional beings. You understand the importance of relying on intuition to figure out your spiritual path and help others awaken to who they are.

Pleiadian lightworkers bring balance and harmony to different energies. This means that you can sense when there is disharmony in the room. You can tell when there's something that is energetically off. Also, you are remarkable at diffusing tension and bringing things back to equilibrium. This is because you are a natural healer; all relationships and situations stand to benefit from your presence in or around them.

As a Pleiadian lightworker, you are responsible for unity consciousness and collective collaboration. You know that the ultimate purpose of the lightworker can only be fulfilled by working with everyone. Therefore, you are particular about encouraging cooperation and support whenever you can.

Being a Pleiadian lightworker means you have multidimensional awareness. In other words, you are open to perspectives of which most people are unaware. Also, you are aware of other realms and dimensions of existence. You can go to these realms and work your way through them to gain wisdom and connect with the higher-dimensional occupants of that realm. Whatever you glean from that realm is something you can bring back to Earth for its greatest good.

The final characteristic of the Pleiadian lightworker is a deep respect and reverence for the Earth. This means you are very passionate about keeping the environment sustainable. You want to ensure that the world remains a green one. You realize the importance of balance and harmony between nature and humanity. And you are unafraid to do what is necessary to ensure that balance remains intact or at least as much of it is preserved as possible.

Do understand that these traits also apply to lightworkers from other star systems besides the Pleiades. However, these are often associated with lightworkers from the Pleiadian star system. If you feel confused about where to start, ask your guides for help. You may need to refer to the previous chapter to find the best modality for you to do so.

Can I Be a Lightworker Regardless of My Religion?

Some argue that lightworking is not something you should do if you're from certain religious backgrounds. These people claim that certain religious doctrines have teachings that do not fit with lightworking ideas. For instance, they point out that since you must worship a deity and no one else, you cannot engage with other spiritual ideas.

Another point to consider is that there are religions that insist there's only one true path: theirs. They cannot possibly fathom that there could be any other path to spiritual enlightenment or salvation. Because of this exclusive attitude, it is impossible for these people even to consider working with teachings and practices from other spiritual philosophies.

There's also the matter of syncretism to consider: the integration of various belief systems to form an entirely new one. This is the same way African religions had been syncretized to create new ones to escape detection from their colonial masters. Those who argue that syncretism is a threat are worried because they see lightworking as a disrespectful combination of different spiritual paths.

Yet another argument against practicing lightworking is that some traditions are strict about sticking to certain religious rituals, dogmas, and leaders. In other words, religions like these do not allow intuition or individual self-reflection. As lightworking is a practice that requires checking in with yourself and following your intuition, these religions, they argue, do not line up with lightworking.

However, having raised all these points, you must remember that lightworking is something everyone can do regardless of their religious background. For one thing, lightworking is based on universal principles. These principles include healing, love, passion, and service. How could these principles be the antithesis of other religions? These principles happen to be a common theme across all religions. Lightworking is simply the amplification and expansion of these principles.

Another thing is that spiritual journeys are a matter of personal interpretation. This means that religious beliefs, while seemingly objective, will be interpreted subjectively. Lightworking allows you to bring together different aspects of various religions to find something true to you. At the end of the day, regardless of your religious affiliation, your practice will always be personal.

Another reason it's okay for you to be a lightworker regardless of your religious background is that lightworking is about spiritually important themes and not rigid dogmas. Being a lightworker means you understand that there are multiple ways to grow spiritually – no one religion has the ultimate "path to salvation." The lightworker chooses to celebrate other paths rather than denigrate them.

As a lightworker, your focus is on unity and oneness. In other words, you recognize that every religion has one goal: love. Every religion wants people to evolve spiritually to greater heights. And every religion would like to see humanity exist in harmony. Therefore, being a lightworker is an invitation to move past religious boundaries and divisions so that individuals can come together as a collective.

A final point to consider about why you can and should be a lightworker is that it will empower you to connect directly with the wisdom and guidance within you. Lightworking is all about encouraging change on a personal level. You will be more driven to be proactive in your spiritual evolution. For these reasons and many more, if you discover you are a Pleiadian Starseed, you should embrace your duty fully, regardless of which religion you were born into.

Lightworking Techniques

You can use the following lightworking techniques to play your part as a lightworker.

Healing and Transformation Meditation

1. First, find somewhere comfortable and quiet where you will not be disturbed or distracted for at least 10 to 15 minutes.
2. Sit or lie down, shut your eyes, and bring your attention to your breath. Take a few deep breaths to allow your mind to unwind and your body to relax.
3. In your mind's eye, see a radiant, golden light that floats above you. This light is divine.
4. Notice this light descending slowly towards you and coming into your body through the crown of your head. Allow this light to flow from your head to every cell of your body. Notice this light energizing your energy centers from your crown chakra to your root chakra.
5. Feel this energy as it cleanses your entire body and mind. Also, allow it to give you fresh energy to take on anything.
6. Intend to allow this light to continue healing and changing you as needed. Intend for the light to flow to any part of your body that needs to be healed. You can also channel this light to aspects of your psyche that require transformation and healing.
7. You may remain in this state of meditation for as long as you like before you finally end with gratitude and come out of it.

Visualization for Divine Light and Positive Outcomes

1. Find a quiet and comfortable place where you can sit without any distractions.
2. Shut your eyes and breathe deeply for a few breaths to ground and center yourself.
3. In your mind's eye, imagine a brilliant, pure light that comes down from the sky. Allow this light to enter your body through the crown chakra.
4. Notice this divine light as it flows through your body. Feel it as it makes your body lighter and cleaner, energetically and otherwise.

5. Now, if there is a situation that you would like to resolve or a person you would like to help, bring them to your mind. Envision this divine light enveloping the situation or person. As the light circles them, it fixes everything that needs to be sorted out.
6. Imagine that this light imbues the situation or person with positive healing energy.
7. You may continue to hold this vision for as long as you feel necessary, and when you're ready to come out of it, be sure to express gratitude to the energies that have helped you.

Channeling Physical, Emotional, and Spiritual Healing

1. Start by grounding and centering yourself with deep breaths.
2. Set an intention to connect with divine light that will bring healing.
3. Put both hands on whichever part of your body needs healing. If you're not working on yourself, put your hands over whomever you're helping with healing.
4. Shut your eyes and imagine that the divine light flows through both your hands and into this area of the body. This divine light is pure healing energy. It helps to see this light as a beautiful emerald green.
5. Understand that you are serving as a channel for this divine light. In other words, you must trust that the light knows where to go and how to act on the body part that needs healing.
6. Remain in this state for as long as you like until you intuitively sense it is time to end the session. While in this state, you must continue to see the divine energy pouring out of your hands and into the body part.
7. Come out of it by expressing gratitude. Understand that what you have done will bring real, positive change. So, rather than look for signs that what you did worked, trust the process, and let things go.

Positive Affirmations for Alignment with Divinity and Reinforcing Positive Beliefs

1. Take out your journal and take some time to craft positive affirmations in line with your intentions and desires.

2. Go somewhere comfortable and quiet where you can repeat these affirmations out loud over and over to yourself. Note that if you do not want to repeat them out loud, you can say them over and over again in your mind.

3. Center yourself by breathing deeply for a few breaths and bring your attention to the here and now.

4. When you feel centered and grounded, begin to repeat your affirmations. You should feel the energy of them as you speak them. In other words, you must mean each word you say.

5. Allow the feeling of truth and power in your affirmations to overwhelm you. If you're doing it right, every cell of your being will buzz with excitement.

6. Make these affirmations a daily habit. You're going to need more than one session to make them stick. Ideally, never stop making these affirmations. Even after you have achieved your goal, you should continue using these affirmations.

A Simple Gratitude Exercise

1. First thing in the morning, take some time to think about the abundance in your life. There are so many ways in which you are blessed consistently. Give yourself time, and things will begin to float into your awareness.

2. Now, find a nice quiet place to sit in comfort and focus.

3. Close your eyes. Breathe in deeply a few times so you can feel grounded and centered.

4. Now, recall everything for which you are thankful. It doesn't matter how insignificant you think it is. Just be thankful.

5. As you inhale and exhale, allow the feeling of gratitude to fill you from head to toe. Pay attention to how your heart feels as you let this feeling of thankfulness and joy flood your entire being.

6. Allow yourself to be overcome by the feeling of appreciation for all the good that has come into your life.

7. Alternatively, you can express your thanks by journaling, using a gratitude list, or saying "thank you" repeatedly.

Understand that regardless of the techniques you choose, they are all effective. There is no hard and fast rule about how you should use them. If you feel drawn to combine several of them, do that. Once more, it is worth repeating that you can modify them according to your beliefs or in line with what your intuition asks you to do in the moment of practice. Either way, you are going to get phenomenal results.

Conclusion

Finally, you have come to the end of this book. If you have been paying attention and chosen to integrate the message herein, then the knowledge, insights, and practices you have gained will cause radical change within you. By choosing to be a part of the Pleiadian exploration of spirituality, you will find more of who you are. You will experience healing, too. You will also find that the awakening never ends. This path that you walk is one that you should be honored to be on.

All through this book, you have learned everything there is to know about Pleiadian teachings. You've come to learn about their cosmic roots, the principles that they hold dear, as well as the insightful messages that humanity urgently needs to hear.

Odds are, you have come to learn about your connection to the Pleiadian race, their energy, and how these things affect your soul's evolution. Now, you should be able to recognize the Pleiadian energies that surround and support you. By delving even deeper into Pleiadian spirituality, you will experience an expansion in your consciousness.

You, brave soul, have opened yourself up to incredible possibilities of cosmic truths and higher realms beyond anything you could imagine. You will discover in practical terms the power of compassion, unity, and love in your life and the lives of those around you. These are the underpinnings of Pleiadian teachings that will help you recall the divinity that lies within you. Never again will you forget that you are part of the all.

This book has equipped you with various techniques, tools, and spiritual practices which support your journey. With these tools, you will discover who you are and finally live in alignment with your soul's true purpose. From choosing to work with Pleiadian guides, discovering sacred geometry, and learning about light languages that help you activate the dormant DNA within you, your life is about to change exponentially. This is because, whether you realize it yet or not, you have just tapped into the powerful, transformative Pleiadian energies, and they will give you all you need to embrace your spiritual potential. The positive changes you will manifest in your life and the world around you will seem daunting, but when you get used to it, *the magic happens.*

Having mapped out the path from one star to the other in the Pleiades system in the pages of this book, you must understand that the power of the knowledge you have gained is not in simply having it in your head but in applying it practically. Do not let this be some intellectual pursuit. Being a Pleiadian Starseed is about experiencing what that means. It will be a personal journey full of challenges, but it's worth it. Working with Pleiadian spirituality is an invitation from your soul as it asks you to explore the treasures it holds in store for you. It is about connecting you to the energies of light, love, and harmony every day.

May everything you've learned in this book resonate deeply in your soul and lead you to the next level in your spiritual journey. May you be empowered to fully and confidently embody the energy of creating spirituality in every aspect of your life. Always remember who you are: a radiant, beautiful being, full of light, capable of making so many powerful shifts within yourself and in the world at large.

Every human has essential and distinct parts to play. As a Pleiadian Starseed, you have been summoned to shine so bright that everyone sees you. This means you must wake up to the truth about who you are to become an agent of positive transformation on the earth. Therefore, you are being asked to make peace with your innate gifts and share them with everyone. This way, you can create a reality full of harmony and enlightenment.

So, dearest Pleiadian Starseed, may the Pleiadian energies ever guide you. May they ever nurture you in all your ways. May they leave you feeling inspired as you go about your spiritual journey. May you ever remember you are a divine being and that in your heart are infinite possibilities for greatness. May the wisdom, light, and love of the Seven Sisters of the Heavens always permeate your life.

Glossary

Activation: This is the unlocking of dormant abilities that a human has.

Age of Aquarius: An astrological epoch that leads to the awakening of collective consciousness.

Ascension: Raising consciousness to become even more aware.

Awakening: Becoming aware of the larger part of one's self and that there's more to life and existence than one was previously aware of. It is gaining consciousness of other dimensions of existence and the soul.

Chakras: Also known as energy centers, they keep the body's energetic system working as it should and can be used as portals to channel energy from higher consciousness.

Channeling: A process that involves the transmission of messages from beings from other dimensions through a human, known as a *channel* to others.

Consciousness: The awareness of being, which permeates everything and every being in existence, known and unknown.

Divine Blueprint: The template of the soul meant to be expressed through one's life.

Energetic cleansing: The clearing of one's natural energy field to eradicate low vibrational energies and allow easy ascension and consciousness expansion.

Intuition: Guidance from within or from other higher-dimensional beings.

Light language: An energy-based language requiring frequencies, sounds, and symbols, which can cause shifts in consciousness.

Lightworker: A person who works with higher-dimensional intelligence and energies to help the world heal and ascend in consciousness.

Pleiadian astrology: Astrology used in conjunction with Pleiadian wisdom.

Pleiadian Guides: These are Pleiadians whoPleiadians offer humans their support, guidance, and wisdom in spiritual affairs.

Pleiadians: Beings who come from the Pleiadian star system with powerful spiritual and cosmic knowledge to share with humanity and the rest of the cosmos.

Sacred Geometry: Shapes that form the building blocks of life and possess unique energies for various purposes.

Soul mission: The mission a soul is supposed to accomplish in this world and lifetime.

Starseed: A soul who used to be part of a star system (like Pleiades, Orion, etc.) who has incarnated on Earth to help humanity expand its consciousness.

If you enjoyed this book, I'd greatly appreciate a review on Amazon because it helps me to create more books that people want. It would mean a lot to hear from you.

To leave a review:
1. Open your camera app.
2. Point your mobile device at the QR code.
3. The review page will appear in your web browser.

Thanks for your support!

Here's another book by Mari Silva that you might like

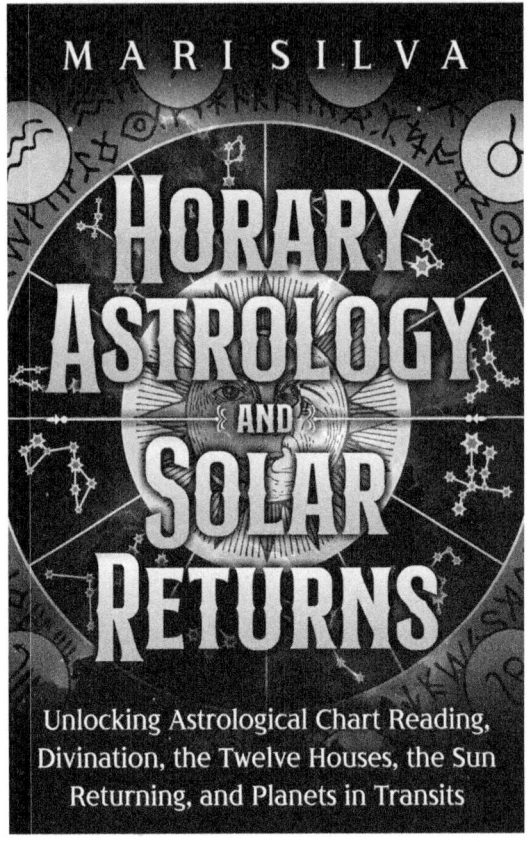

Your Free Gift
(only available for a limited time)

Thanks for getting this book! If you want to learn more about various spirituality topics, then join Mari Silva's community and get a free guided meditation MP3 for awakening your third eye. This guided meditation mp3 is designed to open and strengthen ones third eye so you can experience a higher state of consciousness. Simply visit the link below the image to get started.

https://spiritualityspot.com/meditation

Or, Scan the QR code!

References

Beaconsfield, H. (1998). Welcome to Planet Earth: A guide for walk-ins, Starseeds, and lightworkers of all varieties. Light Technology Publications.

Evans, W. J. (2021). Beginner's guide to Starseeds: Understanding star people and finding your own origins in the stars. Adams Media Corporation.

Fennell, A.-S. (2015). Starseeds of divine matrix. inspirational messages from enlightened beings. Lulu Press, Inc.

Gaughan, D. (2019). Star bred prophecy: A story of star people and Starseeds awakening. Independently Published.

Hoskins, R. S. (2012). For Starseeds: Healing the heart-pleiadian crystal meditations. Balboa Press.

Lanman, A. (2019). Conscious awakening: A research compendium for Starseeds wanderers and lightworkers. BookBaby.

Lewis, B. (2018). Star beings: Their mission and prophecy. Createspace Independent Publishing Platform.

Shaman, M. T., Pestano, M., Juan, A., Lopez, M., & Bliss, S. (2019). Awakening Starseeds: Shattering Illusions vol. 1. Independently Published.

Shurka, J., Finkel, L., Messner, S., Hopkins, P. W., & Seckinger, C. (2022). Awakening Starseeds: Dreaming into the future. Radhaa Publishing House.

Sim, G. (2019). Finding yourself for Starseeds and lightworkers: Activations from 7 star races for reawakening to your galactic presence. Independently Published

Bekbassar, N. (2002). Astronomy in Kazakh Folk Culture. Paper presented at the SEAC 2002 Tenth Annual Conference, Tartu, Estonia.

Bekbassar, N. (2007). Pleiades in the Kazakh Ethnoastronomy. Paper presented at the 15th Annual Meeting of the European Society for Astronomy in Culture, Klaipėda, Lithuania, July 22-31, 2007.

CrystalWind.ca. (n.d.). The 12 Divine Pleiadian Laws - Pleiadian Light Forces. http://www.crystalwind.ca/starseed-messages/the-pleiadians/the-12-divine-pleiadian-laws-pleiadian-light-forces

Fey, T. (2022, June 5). What is a Pleiadian starseed? 29 powerful signs you are one. Nomadrs. https://nomadrs.com/pleiadian-starseed/

Feyerick, A., Gordon, C. H., & Sharma, N. M. (1996). Genesis: World of Myths and Patriarchs. NYU Press. ISBN 0814726682.

Gaia. (n.d.). Am I a Starseed? Types & Characteristics. https://www.gaia.com/article/am-i-a-starseed-types-characteristics

Gibson, S. J. (n.d.). http://www.naic.edu/~gibson

Hand Clow, B. (1995). The Pleiadian Agenda: A New Cosmology for the Age of Light. Santa Fe, NM: Bear and Company Publishing.

Hawkins, G. S., & White, J. B. (1965). Stonehenge Decoded. Doubleday.

https://www.keen.com/articles/astrology/what-is-a-starseed-and-what-does-it-mean-in-astrology

Japingka Aboriginal Art. (n.d.). Star Dreaming - Seven Sisters. https://japingkaaboriginalart.com/articles/star-dreaming-seven-sisters/

Keen. (n.d.). What is a Starseed and What Does it Mean in Astrology?

Korff, K. K. (2010). Spaceships of the Pleiades. Prometheus Books.

Marciniak, B. (2010). Path of empowerment: New Pleiadian wisdom for a world in chaos. New World Library.

Massey, G. (1998). The Natural Genesis. Black Classic Press. ISBN 1574780093.

Mayastar Academy. (n.d.). Pleiadian DNA Clearing & Activation Course. https://www.mayastar.net/pleiadiandna.htm

Monique Chapman. (n.d.). Pleiadian Earth Astrology. https://moniquechapman.com/pleiadian-earth-astrology/

Muller, W. M. (2004). Egyptian Mythology. Kessinger Publishing.

Murphy, A., & Moore, R. (2008). Island of the Setting Sun: In Search of Ireland's Ancient Astronomers. Liffey Press. www.mythicalireland.com

Natural History Museum. (n.d.). Are we really made of stardust? https://www.nhm.ac.uk/discover/are-we-really-made-of-stardust.html

Orleane, P. S., & Smith, C. B. (2013). Conversations with Laarkmaa: A Pleiadian View of the New Reality. Balboa Press.

Partridge, C. (2015). Channeling extraterrestrials: Theosophical discourse in the space age. In Handbook of Spiritualism and Channeling (pp. 390-417). Brill.

Pleiades Observing Project. (n.d.). http://www.ast.cam.ac.uk/~ipswich/Observations/Pleiades_Observing_Proj/POP.htm

Pleiadian Family. (n.d.). How to Contact Pleiadians - Part 1: The App. https://www.pleiadianfamily.net/post/how-to-contact-pleiadians-part-1-the-app

Rappenglück, M. A. (1999). Earth, Moon, and Planets, 85(86), 391-404. doi:10.1023/A:1006216413733

Ruggles, C. L. N. (2005). Ancient Astronomy. ABC-Clio. ISBN 1851094776.

Salla, M. E. (2005). A Report on the Motivations and Activities of Extraterrestrial Races-. Exopolitics. Org.

Sinclair, R. M. (2005). The Nature of Archaeoastronomy. In J. W. Fountain & R. M. Sinclair (Eds.), Current Studies in Archaeoastronomy (ISBN 0890897719).

Think About It. (n.d.). The Pleiadians. https://thinkaboutit.site/aliens/the-pleiadians/

Windows to the Universe. (n.d.). Krittika (Pleiades). https://www.windows2universe.org/mythology/Krittika_pleiades.html

Image Sources

[1] https://www.pexels.com/photo/man-praying-under-the-tree-4049004/

[2] https://pixabay.com/photos/thor-dramatic-fantasy-mystical-4225949/

[3] Photo by Надя Кисільова on Unsplash https://unsplash.com/photos/woman-in-brown-long-sleeve-shirt-and-black-pants-sitting-on-white-textile-QiYZCKJQMck

[4] David (Deddy) Dayag, CC BY-SA 4.0 <https://creativecommons.org/licenses/by-sa/4.0>, via Wikimedia Commons: https://commons.wikimedia.org/wiki/File:Andromeda_Galaxy_560mm_FL.jpg

[5] Dylan O'Donnell, deography.com, CC0, via Wikimedia Commons: https://commons.wikimedia.org/wiki/File:M45_The_Pleiades_Seven_Sisters.jpg

[6] https://commons.wikimedia.org/wiki/File:Sirius_A_and_B_artwork.jpg

[7] https://www.pexels.com/photo/adult-biology-chemical-chemist-356040/

[8] https://www.pexels.com/photo/hands-over-fortune-telling-crystal-ball-7179804/

[9] https://www.pexels.com/photo/concentrated-young-multiethnic-friends-with-map-in-railway-station-6140458/

[10] Roberto Mura, CC BY-SA 4.0 <https://creativecommons.org/licenses/by-sa/4.0>, via Wikimedia Commons: https://commons.wikimedia.org/wiki/File:Arcturus_DSS.png

[11] Morigan221, CC BY-SA 3.0 <https://creativecommons.org/licenses/by-sa/3.0>, via Wikimedia Commons: https://commons.wikimedia.org/wiki/File:Vega_-_star_in_Lyra.png

[12] https://www.pexels.com/photo/studio-shot-of-mother-and-daughter-hugging-17049338/

[13] https://www.pexels.com/photo/eye-looking-at-the-camera-3712574/

[14] Christopher Michel, CC BY 3.0 <https://creativecommons.org/licenses/by/3.0>, via Wikimedia Commons: https://commons.wikimedia.org/wiki/File:The_North_Pole_(139653149).jpeg

[15] https://www.pexels.com/photo/notes-on-board-3782142/

[16] https://unsplash.com/photos/cXVkDKZ_ikE

[17] https://unsplash.com/photos/9wH624ALFQA

[18] https://www.pexels.com/photo/silhouette-of-people-stargazing-2901134/

[19] https://commons.wikimedia.org/wiki/File:Consciousness_phenomenal-functional_(en).png

[20] https://www.pexels.com/photo/group-of-people-holding-arms-461049/

[21] https://unsplash.com/photos/TbuescuqMjA

[22] https://www.pexels.com/photo/meditating-woman-standing-in-front-of-a-projection-6932066/

[23] Till Credner, CC BY-SA 3.0 <https://creativecommons.org/licenses/by-sa/3.0>, via Wikimedia Commons: https://commons.wikimedia.org/wiki/File:AquariusCC.jpg

[24] Image by Victoria from Pixabay https://pixabay.com/photos/dna-biology-the-science-dna-helix-7090994/

[25] Fred the Oyster, CC BY-SA 4.0 <https://creativecommons.org/licenses/by-sa/4.0>, via Wikimedia Commons: https://commons.wikimedia.org/wiki/File:Astrological_Chart_--_New_Millennium.svg

[26] https://unsplash.com/photos/vs-PjCh5goo

[27] NASA Goddard Space Flight Center from Greenbelt, MD, USA, CC BY 2.0 <https://creativecommons.org/licenses/by/2.0>, via Wikimedia Commons: https://commons.wikimedia.org/wiki/File:Hubble_Peers_into_the_Storm_(29563971405).jpg

[28] CC0 Public Domain https://www.publicdomainpictures.net/en/view-image.php?image=151336&picture=flower-of-life

[29] Image by Victoria from Pixabay https://pixabay.com/illustrations/meditation-spiritual-yoga-zen-6988318/

[30] https://www.pexels.com/photo/women-sitting-on-black-chairs-facing-each-other-while-having-a-conversation-9065326/

[31] https://unsplash.com/photos/e3jKBZoRnTs

Printed in Great Britain
by Amazon

57406674R00119